The 30-Day Small Business Startup Plan:
Find Out if You Have What it Takes to Be Your Own Boss
and Achieve Financial Freedom

By

Sam Kerns

Copyright © 2018 Sam Kerns. All rights reserved.

Books by Sam Kerns

How to Work from Home and Make Money: 10 Proven Home-Based Businesses You can Start Today (Work from Home Series: Book 1)

How to Build a Writing Empire in 30 Days or Less (Work from Home Series: Book 2)

How to Start a Home-Based Food Business: Turn Your Foodie Dreams into Serious Income (Work from Home Series: Book 3)

How to Brand Your Home-Based Business: Why Business Branding is Crucial for Even the Smallest Startups (Work from Home Series: Book 4)

How to Publish a Book on Amazon: Real Advice from Someone Who's Doing it Well (Work from Home Series: Book 5)

The Writer's Toolbox Boxed Set (Work from Home Series)

The Weekend Writer: How to Write a Non-Fiction Book in 2 Months, Even if You Have a Full-Time Job (Work from Home: Book 6)

How to Relaunch Your Book: Use This Step-By-Step Proven Program to Bring Your Book Back to Life (Work from Home: Book 7)

The 30-Small Business Startup Plan : Find Out if You Have What it Takes to Be Your Own Boss and Achieve Financial Success (Work from Home: Book 8)

Sign up at RainMakerPress.com to receive advanced notice of new books in the series!

Contents

Introduction: There are Challenges, But Don't Be Discouraged	6
Part One: Do You Have the Personality Traits and Skills to Be Your Own Boss? (And What to Do About it if You Don't.)	12
Part Two: Do You Have a Product or Service That People Want to Buy? (How to Know and What to Do About It if You Don't.)	36
Part Three: Do You Have Enough Money to Start This Business? (How to Know and What to Do About it if You Don't.)	49
Part Four: Putting it All Together, Creating a Roadmap for Success, and a Surprise Ending	73
How to Work From Home and Make Money: 10 Proven Home-Based Businesses You Can Start Today (Work from Home Series: Book 1)	80
How to Build a Writing Empire in 30 Days or Less (Work from Home Series: Book 2)	82
How to Start a Home-Based Food Business: Turn Your Foodie Love into Serious Cash with a Food Business Startup (Work from Home Series Book 3)	84
How to Brand Your Home-Based Business: Why Business Branding is Crucial for Even the Smallest Startups (Work from Home Series Book 4)	86
The Writer's Toolkit Boxed Set (Work from Home: Books 2 and 5)	88
The Weekend Writer: How to Write a Non-Fiction Book in Two Months even if You Have a Full-Time Job (Work from Home Series: Book 6)	89
How to Relaunch Your Book: Use this 7-Step Proven Program to Bring Your Book Back to Life (Book 7)	90

Read my books for FREE by signing up for my mailing list! Click here or go to RainMakerPress.com

Introduction: There are Challenges, But Don't Be Discouraged

Disclaimer: This chapter is not meant to bum you out. Some of the facts and figures quoted in it are dismal, and I debated about whether or not I should open the book with them. But the point of this book is to illustrate the importance of examining yourself and your idea before you take the life-altering step of starting a business—and then doing what you can to mitigate the risks. You see, I believe the old cliché is correct: knowledge is power. If you don't understand the risks up front, you won't see the importance of preparation.

So read this chapter with a strong heart and know that in subsequent chapters I will show you how to overcome these odds and go on to start a successful business.

Are you ready to see if you've got what it takes to be your own boss? Let's get started.

Quick—what's your number one priority as a would-be entrepreneur? If you're like most people your answer falls somewhere in the following responses:

- To make as much money as I can
- To create a product or service that benefits people and makes their lives easier
- To be my own boss
- To work my own hours
- To escape the rat race
- To leave a financial legacy to my family

Although these are lofty goals, none of them should be your number one priority when thinking about starting a business. Certainly some of you have these goals, as you should, but before you can begin thinking about making a lot of money or quitting your 9 to 5, there is only one thing you should be focusing on:

To prepare as much as possible before launching in order to ensure success

It's not as sexy as the previously listed goals I know, but the truth is that you can have the best intentions and the most innovative and disruptive business concept and still fail. How? By jumping in feet first instead of properly analyzing your idea and preparing yourself for entrepreneurship.

Don't believe me? Here are 2 sobering statistics about small business failures:

- According to the Labor of Statistics, only about 50 percent of new businesses are still open after the first year.
- According to Small Business Trends, only 40 percent of small businesses earn a profit, 30 percent of them just break even, and a sad 30 percent of them are losing money.

That means out of all the people who started a business just a year ago, only half of them are still open and of those, only 40 percent earn a profit. And the other half? Despite all their hopes, best intentions and efforts, they had to say goodbye to their dream and close the doors to their business.

Sad, isn't it?

But instead of looking at the grim statistics and becoming pessimistic about your chances for a successful business, let's take a look at some other numbers that will help shed some light on the topic. For example, some recent studies show these startling facts:

- According to a survey conducted by Small Business Trends, over half of the people asked say the best way to learn about entrepreneurship is to start a business. In other words, they don't understand the necessity of research and preparation when starting a business. They think they can "learn as they go." I can only guess that this type of thinking about starting a business is why the failure rate is so high.
- Forty-six percent of all small business failures are attributed to incompetence. In other words, the people who started the small business didn't do their homework or prepare before they took the leap.

- Thirty percent of small business failures comes from a lack of managerial experience or an "unbalanced" experience. That means the 30 percent of those who failed in these instances were so in love with their business idea they didn't take the time to understand what was required for success before opening their business.
- Thirteen percent of small business failures were due to neglect, fraud, or disaster. In short, that means these entrepreneurs failed to identify potential weaknesses in their plan before launching, or didn't hire the right team members. My hunch is that most of these closures could have been avoided with the exception of those closing because of a disaster.
- Eleven percent of small business closures happened because the founder had a lack of experience in that type of service or goods. Does a lack of preparation get any more obvious than this?

These numbers looked at individually are shocking, but what's even more so is looking at them as a whole. Let me illustrate what they mean in an easy-to-understand graphic:

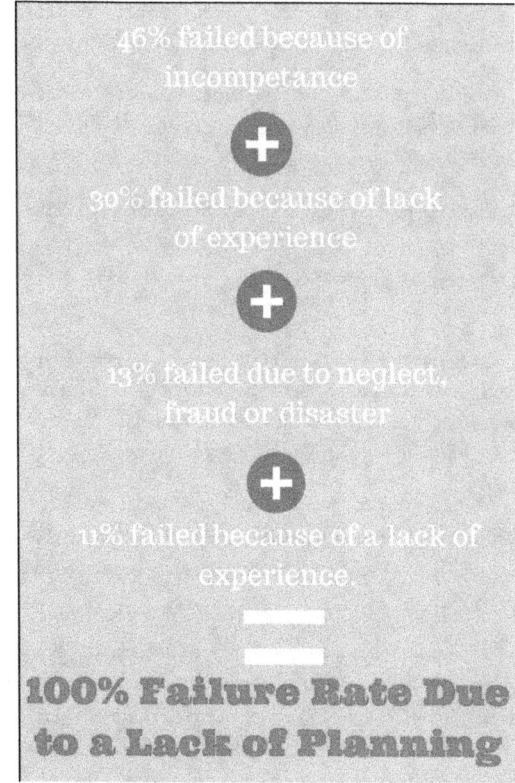

Do you see where I'm going with this?

Yes, the small business failure rates are dismal, but when we look at the reasons why half of all new businesses fail within the first year, things begin to look a bit more optimistic, don't they? Almost 100 percent (minus those that closed because of a disaster) of businesses that failed might have gone on to be a success if only the owners had spent more time planning and less time dreaming before they opened their doors.

Don't get me wrong, I believe in dreams. **But dreams are just wishes unless they're paired with sufficient knowledge and action.** But boy, when you combine a great dream with enough planning, the possibilities are endless.

Starting a new business is serious work, but it can also be one of the most rewarding, life-changing, and exciting ventures of your life. But as you can see from the figures above, not everyone approaches this epic event in a way that leads to a successful and profitable business.

If you're planning to start your own business, shouldn't you do it in a way that gives you the best chance of success? After all, we're talking about your dream aren't we? You can either approach it haphazardly like the 50 percent of people who failed, or do it in a thoughtful, planned-out way that almost always results in success.

That's what this book is all about. I'll start by asking you to take a good look at yourself to identify the strengths, weaknesses, traits, and habits that will most likely help you or hurt you—and then show you how to take some steps to rectify any hindrances you uncover.

Next, we'll look at your business product or idea, financial situation, and long-term goals and then consolidate everything you learn in an easy-to-use worksheet. In this 30-day process, you will use the startup roadmap in a strategic and methodical way that will tell you realistically whether you should launch your new business now—or if you need to spend a little more time in the planning stages.

And that's priceless information, don't you think?

If you're going to start your own business, don't take the leap before doing all you can to ensure your success. Reading this book—and following the principles outlined in it—is a great way to make sure you don't end up as one of the 50 percent of people who didn't plan and prepare enough before launching their business.

Are you ready to analyze your business idea? Let's move on and talk about the personality traits, characteristics, habits, and skills most entrepreneurs have and why. We'll use an evaluation method to determine if you're really well-suited for life as a business owner. (And what to do if you're not.)

Part One: Do You Have the Personality Traits and Skills to Be Your Own Boss? (And What to Do About it if You Don't.)

Owning your own business is the hardest job you'll ever have. While it's true that there are countless benefits to running your own business, no one who is being honest will tell you that it's easy. That's because as a business owner, you can't rely on anyone else to do what needs to get done. If a client needs to spend an hour on the phone on Christmas Day because that's the only day he has free, you better plan to take the time to talk to him. If there is a client presentation that has to be done today and your virtual assistant is out sick, you'll need to find the time to do it. If the sidewalk that leads to your office needs to be shoveled to remove the snow and no one else is around, you'll need to pull out your boots. In other words, as a business owner, you are responsible for everything that happens (or doesn't happen) in your company.

It takes a special kind of person to run and manage a business, and not everyone is cut out for it.

I'd like to start by talking about some non-negotiable traits and skills that entrepreneurs need in order to be successful, and then I'll add a few of my own that so many people overlook. In each section, I'll ask you analyze yourself to see if you possess them. And if you find that you don't, I'll give you some free resources to help you develop and improve them.

Please use a notebook or your keyboard and keep track of your answers—you'll need them to conduct your personal evaluation.

Traits Every Entrepreneur Must Have

The following are traits and skills that are non-negotiable for anyone who wants to start a business. Be honest in your evaluation of yourself and if you recognize any that you lack, look to the resources I provide to help develop them.

A Great Work Ethic

I began with this because in my opinion, having a great work ethic is the most important personal trait you need when starting your own business. Like I said above, running your own business is the most difficult job you'll ever have and if you're someone who is used to taking shortcuts or quitting before a task or project is complete, you may not be cut out for the life as a business owner.

Let me illustrate this with a scenario: Imagine that you run a newly started commercial landscaping company, and a group of business owners asks you to give a presentation and collective bid for your services. Their requirements are steep and the presentation will take hours to prepare. In addition, you'll need to visit each owner's property and then complete an individual bid for all of them. The potential is huge, and getting the bulk contract could bring in some much needed cash flow to your fledgling business. But the group has only given you a week to prepare.

It is a series of crucial junctures like these that determine whether or not a person is cut out to be an entrepreneur. Someone who is will begin work on the project right away in case they run into unexpected roadblocks or problems. They will not only meet the deadline, but the presentation they give will be thoughtful and thorough, and the bid will be justifiable and in line with the competition. This type of person will likely go on to create a successful business.

But someone who procrastinates, who would ask for an extension on the deadline, or worse, would never get around to doing it is doomed from the start.

And here's where it gets tricky. I imagine that about 99.9 percent of those reading this book are thinking that they would never, ever pass up an opportunity like that, and would do all it takes to make their business a success. But if that's true, why do so many businesses fail due to neglect and lack of motivation? The answer is clear: even those people who don't have a great work ethic *believe* they will behave differently in their new business. Unfortunately, the statistics just don't back up that belief.

The Assessment: We're going to take the wishing and good intentions out of the equation when it comes to your work ethic. I want you to think about the past 6 months of your life and quickly, without much thought, jot down the 4 biggest events that occurred. It could be an important task at work, a job interview, a move, a relationship issue or some other event.

Now, think back to how you handled the details of it. If you had an important job interview, did you take the time to prepare for it or did you wait until the last minute and then just wing it? If you moved recently, did you pack up well in advance, or were you still stuffing things into boxes when the movers showed up? If you had a relationship issue and needed to work things out with your significant other, did you sit down and discuss it before things spiraled out of control, or did you keep putting it off until things got ugly? What about that important task you were assigned at work? Did you take the time to get it done right and on time, or did you just squeak by and do as little as possible?

How you reacted to these events in your life are all indicators of your work ethic. If you can honestly say that you dealt with the issues that came your way head on and in a timely manner, you've got a great advantage. Entrepreneurs who have this trait are much more likely to go on to success.

On the other hand, if you're a procrastinator or someone who takes the easy way out, you're not ready to start and run a business. What can you do about it? Let's talk about some exercises you can do for the next 30 days to help cultivate this entrepreneurial trait.

How to Build a Strong Work Ethic

It is possible to train yourself to have a better work ethic. There are 3 major aspects to a good work ethic and you need to concentrate on all of them. Let's take the next 30 days and form some new habits that will improve your work ethic and get you ready for entrepreneurship. Here's what I would like you to do.

1. **You need to learn to focus.** Part of getting things done is the ability to focus, but too many people try to focus on a lot of things at once. But recent studies show that all that multi-tasking doesn't lead to productivity. For the next 30 days, I want you to do some timed exercises that are aimed at increasing your focus. Whenever you have a task to complete, set a time limit and then focus exclusively

on that task until it's completed. For example, if you need to complete the preliminary research on a work project, set a time limit and focus only on that task until the time is over. If you think 2 hours is sufficient, set a timer for 2 hours and do nothing else until you hear it chime. Doing this for 30 days every time you have a project or task will help retrain your mind to focus.

2. **You need to stop procrastinating.** Procrastination is your enemy as a business owner and it's the reason so many new businesses fail. But, just like learning to focus, you can change your inclination toward procrastination. Using the same 30-day method, every time you feel yourself wanting to put something off, force yourself to write down the excuses that are running through your mind. For example, if you need to complete a project and are thinking about putting it off until the morning, write down the reasons why—and then analyze them. Is it because you would rather go to dinner? Then think about whether the dinner or the project will get you closer to your dreams and then make a decision. Is it because you're tired? Write that down and then ask yourself if you're too tired to complete a simple project, how will you have enough energy to run a business? The only way this method will work is if you are brutally honest with yourself and then take action on what you find. Do this for 30 days, and if at the end of it you have a tablet full of excuses that you've somehow justified to yourself, you should probably hang onto that 9 to 5 job a little longer. But if you've seen through your excuses and have made some changes, keep at it until your procrastination is a thing of the past.

3. **You need to do your best.** Another part of having a great work ethic is making sure that when you do something, it's done to the best of your ability. And this critical ability to do things right can easily mean the difference between a successful business and a failed one. Let's look at the lawn care business I talked about above as an example. If you were to sloppily put together a presentation, your chances of getting the bid would dramatically decrease. But if you took your time and did the presentation right, it would increase the odds of a yes. If you're in the habit of rushing through things and not doing them the best you can, your business won't survive. To overcome this self-sabotaging trait, you'll need to

develop some new habits. Perhaps the best way to do that is to set a couple of deadlines for every project you undertake. Set one for the work to be done, and then a later deadline for the work to be refined. For example, if you have a work project due in 2 weeks, commit to finishing the draft in a week and a half, and then take the remaining time to refine and perfect the project. Do this consistently for the next 30 days and you'll quickly see the difference in how taking the extra time to do things right pays off.

Financial Savvy

I am shocked that so many people have to close their doors because of financial problems. It doesn't surprise me that so many new entrepreneurs have cash flow problems because that can happen in companies run by experts, but to run out of money? That one bowls me over.

If you're going to start a new business, you absolutely must have an idea of how capital works and how to use it for the betterment of your company. We've all heard stories of young, new entrepreneurs who begin doing well and decide to use some of their earnings to buy houses and cars instead of managing their cash flow for long-term growth.

Please, don't let this happen to you. Those kinds of entrepreneurs become statistics, and that's not how you want to end up, do you? There will be plenty of time to buy a house and fancy cars if that's how you want to spend your money, but for the love of all things entrepreneurial, please don't do it prematurely.

That's why it's imperative that if you're going to start a business, you need some financial know-how.

Here are some of the financial skills and knowledge that you should have before you ever open your doors. (And how to learn the skills if you lack them.)

- **You know how to create a budget**. Budgets aren't just for your personal life, you'll also need one for your business. In fact, running a business without one is like driving a car without gas—you just won't be able to get you where you want to go. There is a [free business budgeting tool](#) from Mint.com that you can use in your business as well as your personal life. If you don't already have this skill, it's imperative that you learn it. Start with the [free PDF from SCORE](#) about how to budget for a small business. If you still have questions, go to [Score.org](#) and sign up for a free mentor. You'll be able to meet with one in your local area via email or phone.

- **You can estimate startup costs.** Knowing how to budget for startup costs is also vital to your success. Too many entrepreneurs look at their startup through rose colored glasses and vastly underestimate how much it will cost to get up and running. That's a mistake that could easily lead to a failure before you ever get the chance to get your business off the ground. If you don't know how to estimate startup costs for your new business, you'll need to learn this important skill. You can download a [guide and startup budget template](#) from QuickBooks or a [startup expenses template](#) from SCORE. And again, if you need additional help, call SCORE and speak to a mentor who will help guide you through the process. (I'll also provide an in-depth tutorial in the financial chapter.)

- **You understand cash flow.** Cash flow is the breath in the life of a business. Without it, you won't be able to operate for very long, and if you mismanage it, your business will surely fail. Cash flow is the cash from sales that flow in and out of your business, but too many new entrepreneurs mistake it for profit and spend it. That's a mistake because when it comes time to pay the bills or vendors, there is nothing left in the bank. And that can quickly close down a business. If you don't yet understand the concept of cash flow, you should make it your number one priority in financial matters. You can get a quick start guide at [Study.com](#) where you'll find a free video explaining the concept as well as a quiz to test your current knowledge. In addition, you can download a [free 12 month cash flow statement](#) from SCORE.org. And don't forget to contact a SCORE mentor if you still have questions.

- **You have financial restraint.** In addition to knowing how to best handle cash flow, you will need to exercise financial restraint for the life of your business. You will need to know when to spend it and when it's better to put aside extra cash for future expenditures. In fact, some of the world's most successful entrepreneurs are masters at managing their money. For example, Warren Buffett still lives in the house he bought in 1958. He paid just over $31,000 for that house and never felt the need to upgrade to a more expensive, fancier one. Only you know whether or not you have financial restraint. If you do, you already have an advantage that will be a great benefit to your business. And if you don't? You'll need to set up a system where your spending is checked by someone else. For example, if you decide that you want to purchase a new truck for a service business or some expensive software for an accounting business, you should first run it by your accountant, and then by someone else familiar with your business. If they disagree with you, don't automatically override their opinion. Instead, look at things from their point of view and determine whether or not you can live without the purchase.

- **You understand the basics of business loans.** Unless you have enough cash to invest in your business—or a relative or friend who will loan you the money—you will likely need to take out a loan to get started. Unlike the past when entrepreneurs had to rely on banks to get their startup capital, today's business owners have a lot of options. But all those choices come with various pros and cons, and as a new business owner, you need to understand how each one will affect your business. I wrote a detailed blog post about all the small business loan opportunities out there, which you can find on my Start a Business Blog at rainmakerpress.com.

- **You get the importance of long-range business planning.** In order to build a sustainable business, you need to think long term when it comes to planning. It's not enough to plan for the next 6 months to a year—you should be thinking about years down the road. This type of planning helps take your vision for the business and help make it a reality. And in addition to enabling you to run a more successful business, long-term planning will help you create your exit strategy if that's in the cards for you. A study done by Alternative Board showed that small business owners who have a strategic plan they consider good or excellent are much more likely to experience a sharp increase in profits and sales revenues than owners who don't have one. The key to creating a long-term plan is converting your vision into numbers. You can use free resources like the [3 year profit and loss projection](#) from score.org, and this [3 year cash flow statement](#) from the same site to get started. Remember, the key to long-range planning is to first identify your long-term vision, and then work the numbers to figure out how to make it happen. If you haven't yet identified yours, take some time in the next 30 days and do so. Start by writing down all you want to accomplish in your business and then reduce the points until you come to the core idea. Now, write a paragraph about it, and then reduce it again to 1-2 sentences. This is your long-range plan. You'll need to work your numbers to determine exactly what it will take for you to reach that goal.

How to Build Financial Savvy

In addition to using the resources I outlined in each financial skill that you need to know, you may need to take some basic training to get a deeper understanding of how to financially run a business. Remember, if you don't have control of your finances, it puts your new business at risk.

Luckily, there are some great free online training courses that can help you beef up your knowledge. For example, the [Small Business Association](#) (SBA) offers many courses that can help you get your financial chops in order. In addition, you can take free small business financial courses at [Kutztown University's Small Business Development Center](#) and [Santa Clarita University's My Own Business Institute](#). And whatever courses you decide to take, it would be smart to combine them with a mentor from SCORE who has the experience and a willingness to pass it along to you.

Communication Skills

You can't run a business unless you have the ability to communicate with your customers, employees, vendors, or one of the many people you will come across in your day-to-day affairs. For example, did you know that half of those surveyed in a Gallup poll say they left their job in order to get away from a bad manager? Chances are, those managers didn't have the skills necessary to effectively communicate their desires to the employees.

Here are 4 reasons why you need to have above average communication skills to run a small business. Rate yourself in each one as you read, and decide whether or not you need the (mostly) free resources and learning tools I provide for each one. (Hint: you probably do.)

- **Leadership.** As the owner of a small business, it will fall on your shoulders to motivate your employees and everyone else you come into contact with during the course of your day. You will need to inspire trust, confidence, and a passion for the business in them, and communication will be the way you do it. For example, you may need to motivate your salespeople to perform better while speaking to them at a meeting, instill passion about your business vision in potential vendors at a business show, or cause investors to trust you by reading a written proposal. Do you have leadership skills? If you believe you do, think honestly about the last time you led, and write down the results. Did the people you led willingly follow your lead and perform to the best of their ability? If not, why? If you're not sure, get in contact with them and ask. Tell them you want an honest evaluation of your leadership style and ask for feedback about how you can improve it. If you've never been in a leadership role, think seriously about reading a few books on the topic. My favorite picks are Simon Sinek's _Start with Why_ (or you can watch the Ted Talk for free), or EntreLeadership by Dave Ramsey.
- **Negotiations.** Negotiating will play a huge role in your business activities, and you have to have some pretty serious communication skills in order to do it properly. For example, you'll negotiate with vendors, employees, landlords, customers, and investors and the better you are at striking a deal that's favorable to your business, the better chance of business success you'll have. But there is a fine line between being a tough negotiator and being a jerk, and you'll have to know how to finesse the situation to come out on top. To get a handle on your negotiating style, you can use the free Negotiating Style Assessment Tool at

negotiationplanner.com, where you will also find some other helpful and free tools such as a list of questions that helps develop your negotiating power, and a negotiating performance review tool. In addition, you can read an extensive free guide provided by the Harvard Program on Negotiation. By providing your email when prompted, you'll be able to download this fantastic guide written by experts. Finally, you can take a free Negotiations and Conflict Management Course at Saylor.org. And don't forget to check out my blog at RainMakerPress.com where I've written about the topic and also provide a short video explaining the basic concepts of the art.

- **Sales and Presentations.** Sales and presentations will play a major role in your business, and it's essential that you perfect your ability in both areas. You will use your sales skills every time you come into contact with a potential customer, and will likely be asked to give a presentation about your business a few times a year. These presentations could be similar to our lawn care example above, or you could be asked to give a presentation on a topic aligned with your business, like a lawn care business owner being asked to give a talk at a local homeowner's association about the importance of weed control (And then having the opportunity to sell his services, of course.) And while it's true that every business owner needs these skills, it's also true that so many of them avoid refining them. Why? Because no one wants to seem pushy or too salesy when it comes to their business. Luckily, today's sales aren't the old-school type that browbeats someone into buying something. Today's sales training respects the buyers and simply tries to show them how a product or service can solve a problem for them. To get trained in these important skills, you have a few options. You can take a self-guided free basic sales training course from provensalestraining.com, or get a free sales training course from saleshacker.com. It includes 4 hours of content, 10 videos, and 5 PDFs.

- **Writing.** In some instances, you will need to rely on the written word to get across your ideas or negotiate, so this is another skill you need to be proficient in when running a small business. Even if you never have to put together a written presentation or write a letter to an upset customer or vendor, you will likely have to communicate via email every day. Effective letters, emails, and other forms of written communication are often to-the-point, persuasive, and direct. You will need to be able to get your point across in a way people can understand and you should leave no room for misinterpretation. You can find free online courses such as Study.com's [technical writing course,](#) which includes a chapter on proposal writing, a free 4-week class on [business writing](#) from the University of Colorado, or an excellent [business writing tutorial](#) from Webucator.com. And if you want to check your written communications for spelling and grammar errors, use writing enhancement software like those found at [WhiteSmoke.com](#) ($80 a year) and [ProWritingAid.com](#), where you can use a free limited version, or sign up for a premium account for $50 a year.

Crazy Energy

Remember the Energizer Bunny? He didn't have anything on entrepreneurs, especially in the startup phase of a business. In order to get a new business off the ground, you basically have to suspend every other part of your life. You will live and breathe your new business 24 hours a day. If you thought your boss made you work a lot of hours, just wait until you see the schedule you're going to have to keep in order to grow your baby.

In fact, according to the Bureau of Labor Statistics, people employed by others work an average of 33.8 hour a week but of those who work for themselves , one-third say they work at least 50 hours a week while 25 percent say they work more than 60 hours per week. In addition, 70 percent of all the small business owners surveyed say they typically work at least one weekend. Another survey done by FreeAgent shows that 44 percent of those surveyed say they are unable to get away for a vacation. But even though it's obvious that small business owners work more than those who are employed by others, 74 percent are content with their working life.

In order to grow a new business, you have to put a lot of time and energy into it, and let's be honest, not everyone has that kind of crazy energy. Sure, you can ease up your workload by hiring virtual assistants and other employees, but who do you think will need to manage them? The business owner, that's who.

No assessment is needed to determine whether or not you have the kind of energy it takes to run a business. If you have it, you know, and if you don't, you know that, too. If you already have this kind of energy, congratulate yourself because you can't run a business without it. And if you don't, you will need to make some lifestyle changes and gear up to prepare.

How to Get Crazy Energy

Personally, I use diet, exercise, plenty of sleep, and hydration to keep my energy levels up. I eat consciously and am careful about what I put into my body. I don't eat anything processed, but only whole, real foods that come from the earth, including good proteins and fats. I drink plenty of water all day long. I also juice fresh vegetables and fruits at least once a day and stay away from a lot of carbs and sugar. In addition to eating right, I believe that exercise is one of the key factors in whether or not you have crazy energy. If you need to up your energy levels so you can start a business, changing your lifestyle is, in my opinion, the best thing you can do.

Rather than talk to you about my diet or exercise program, I'll refer you to some resources I trust and believe in. Dr. Josh Axe, GreenMedInfo, and Natural News are great places to learn about how food and exercise affect your everyday life—including your energy levels.

Decision Making Abilities

As the owner of your company, you will be faced with many decisions every day, and you'll need the ability to make the right ones in a timely manner. For example, the decision could be as simple as deciding whether or not to grant a vacation request for one of your employees, or it could be as complex as deciding whether to move your home-based office to a retail setting, if firing the accountant is the right move, or whether or not you should accept a costly proposal from a marketing agency.

Whatever decisions you face, you'll need the ability to logically analyze the situation and make a decision that will best benefit your business.

There are 6 common types of decision making styles—read the list below and see if you recognize yourself in any of them.

- **Opinion Seekers.** Some people want to make decisions based on what a group of involved people believe is right. These people hold meetings a take a vote whenever the company is faced with a decision. The decision of each vote guides the path forward.
- **Relying on Gut.** Some people use their gut reaction as a way to make important business decisions. For example, a real estate investor/landlord may decide who to rent an apartment to based solely on his gut and forego applications and credit checks. People who use this method often have a lot of experience in the matter. If you lack the experience, this can be a dangerous way to make decisions.
- **Data Driven.** On the other hand, some business owners want to look at all the facts and figures before making a decision. They will research and organize the facts and then make a decision based on the reasonable outcome.
- **Prayer.** There are business owners who have a close personal relationship with God who make their decisions after spending time with Him in prayer. For example, the person could ask God for wisdom in making the decision, or for a direct answer about which direction he should take.
- **Making a List.** This method has been around for some time, but there are still some business owners who use it exclusively to make decisions. They first draw a line down the center of the page, and then use the left column for pros and the right for cons. After brainstorming and filling both columns, they look at the results logically and make their decision.
- **Refusing to make decisions.** On the other hand, there are people who will do almost anything to avoid making decisions. These people either don't like making decisions, or are so afraid of making the wrong choice that they become paralyzed. If an employee asks for a raise, they may put off the answer until the employee quits in frustration. If a customer asks for a discount, they may hem-

haw enough that the customer becomes offended and takes their business elsewhere. They may ask others to make decisions for them or covertly coerce others into making decisions de facto.

If you typically make decisions by using the first 5 methods, you're probably right where you need to be in terms of decision-making ability. But if you fall into the last category—someone who refuses to make decisions—you're not ready to start your own business.

How to Learn Decision Making

You cannot successfully start a business until you're comfortable making decisions, period. You will be the one to decide which type of business you're going to start, where you will operate, who to hire, how much to pay them, who to target as clients, which products or services to sell, what to say to customers who want discounts, what your logo looks like, which marketing avenues to purse, or whether or not your employees wear uniforms—and if so, which color. In addition, a leader who cannot effectively make decisions will quickly lose customers and the respect of their employees.

As you can see, people who are unable or unwilling to make decisions are not cut out to run a business. And if you realize that you fall into this category, you'll have to take some steps to build this portion of your character. And seriously, I highly suggest that until you develop the ability to make decisions, you put your entrepreneurial plans on hold.

Here's how you can build this important skill.

The first thing you need to do is decide which of the decision making methods you're more comfortable with. (Keep in mind that for proper decision making, you will likely need to employ more than one method, but there is probably one that you're more comfortable with). Only you can answer this question, but as you look through each method and decide, let me give you a couple of things to think about.

- **You don't want to choose the one that sounds the easiest.** For example, it may sound like going with your gut is easier than researching and looking at all the facts, but in actuality, that depends on the person. For example, if you're an analytical person, trying to listen to your gut—something you can't qualitatively measure—would be torture. Be honest in your evaluation.
- **Know that you may have to use more than one method.** For instance, you may rely on your gut when deciding which marketing campaign to use, but when deciding which employee to promote, you'll likely need to rely on facts and figures.
- **Most decisions are emotional.** It will be impossible to completely remove all emotions when making a decision, and you'll have to factor that into your decision. For example, if you're relying on those facts and figures to determine which employee to promote, your feelings for the employees will also come into play. You may simply get along with one better than the other. In this instance, you'll need to listen to your gut (your emotions) as well as juggle the facts and figures to come up with the best solution for your company.

Now that you've determined your ideal decision making method, let's talk about how you can retrain your brain to make decisions when you need to.

Make Decisions the Right (and Easy) Way

There has been so much written about how to make a decision, and much of it revolves around doing a combination of the decision making methods I listed above.

But there is new research into the subject and some pretty smart people have chimed in on some simple ways of not only making a decision, but how to learn to make the *best* one. Let's talk about some of these methods now.

The Shapiro Method

Ben Shapiro, a former consultant for Bain & Company has come up with a deceptively simple solution for making tough decisions. He says the first step is to ask yourself what you would need in order to believe that the decision is the right one. For example, imagine that you're trying to decide which of 2 employees to promote, and you're leaning towards Jenni, the one that you get along with better.

At this point, you should ask yourself the question. "What do I need to believe that the decision to promote Jenni is the right choice?" Now, you'll need to make a list of assumptions that will help with your decision. In this instance, it could look something like this:

- I believe that Jenni and I will work well together, which will make her better at her job.
- I believe Jenni has the skills to do the job properly.
- I believe Jenni gets along well enough with her co-workers to manage them well.
- I believe Jenni will take the job seriously and give it her all.

Now that you have made a quasi-decision and have a list of assumptions about it, it's time to back it up with a little research and data. For example, you can speak to her current supervisor to understand how well she gets along with her co-workers, check her resume and current job responsibilities to ensure she has the required skills, and then talk to her about the positon and how she feels about it. If everything you find in the fact finding process meets your expectations, you can feel good about the decision. On the other hand, if any of the assumptions are wrong, it's time to take a step back and think hard about the decision. For example, if you learn that Jenni doesn't have the relationship with her co-workers you thought she did, promoting her probably isn't the right decision.

If you can't find data for all of your assumptions, you will have to make an educated guess or keep looking for it. For instance, if you can't find a recent skills list for Jenni, be sure to ask her about it or test her on the important skills before you make a decision.

If your reason for not making decisions lies in the fact that you don't want to make the wrong one, this method should help ease those fears. It follows a course of logic and will likely result in a good decision.

There are a few other expert tips that will help you make good business decisions.

- **Pretend you're giving advice to a friend.** Sometimes you need to take yourself out of the scenario and when you do, it's much easier to see the bigger picture. If you were advising your best friend about which employee you would promote, what would you say? What insights would you give him based on what you've seen?
- **Put it on a spreadsheet.** For all of you analytical types, using a spreadsheet may the impetus that allows you to more easily make decisions. You can download a free decision making tool at LifeHacker.com.
- **Take a free course**. Finally, a little education never hurts, and when it comes to learning how to make decisions, an online course may be all you need to break through the barrier. You can find a free online course called Effective Problem-Solving and Decision-Making at coursera.org.

If decision making isn't something you're good at—or even if it is and you want to practice the methods I talked about in this chapter—take the next 30 days and apply them to every decision you make. It will help to keep a log documenting your successes and failures, and then as you review it, reevaluate your mistakes and learn from them. If you pay close attention to how you make decisions and document the results of them, you will retrain your brain to make the best decisions for you and your business every time.

Passion and Motivation

I've spoken to too many entrepreneurs who tell me that the reason they started their business is to make a lot of money. They didn't necessarily care that much about the product or service, but believed it would create a financial windfall.

For anyone out there who is considering starting a business for the same reason, I have just one question for you: What will keep you going in both good times and bad? Sure, making a lot of money is nice, but over time—as you earn more and more—it's not going to satisfy you, and then you'll have a difficult time staying motivated. And if you don't love your product, business model, or service, you're eventually going to come to resent it.

At the core of every new business owner should be a spark of passion for their business idea, product, or service, and the motivation to get it in front of the public. For example, imagine that there are 2 business owners who have the same idea for a business.

One of them is only in it for the money. He sees a need in the market and is determined to brand a product to fill that need. He spends hours calculating how much money he can make and then dreaming about what he will do with it.

On the other hand, the second entrepreneur has a burning desire to get the product in front of the public because she knows how much people need it. She spends hours imagining how her product is going to change the world, and takes the steps to plan and prepare to launch the product. Of course she wants to make a lot of money from her business, but it's not the only driving factor. She really believes that her new company will make the world a better place.

Now fast forward to 10 years down the road. Both entrepreneurs made a lot of money, but their lives look decidedly different. The person who started the business for the money is stuck at a "job" he hates. He goes to work every day and begrudgingly manages his people and whatever else he has to do so he can leave and do the things he likes. His business has been suffering lately because he isn't managing his cash flow like he knows he should, but dang it, if he has to come to this boring place every day, he may as well get as much from it as he can. So he's diverted some of the cash flow to fund his personal projects and as a result, he's had to lay off some employees. After all, it's his business, he tells himself, and if it goes under, he may as well walk away with as much as he can get.

The second entrepreneur is having a much better time. She is thrilled that her business is doing so well and looks forward to going to work every day to learn how it is changing the lives of her customers. She has hired people to work for her who are just as excited about the product as she is, and they often work overtime because they hate to have to end the day. While her business is thriving, she takes a salary that affords her a great lifestyle, but still reinvests a good portion of it in the business. After all, she wants to pass on the business to her children when she's ready to retire and judging by how well it's doing, it will make for an excellent inheritance.

The entrepreneurs highlighted above are fictional, or course, but represent two paths that business owners can travel down. You have to ask yourself—do you want to be in this for the short term to get a lot of money? If so, you'd better have the ability to motivate yourself for the short term—and then have a solid exit plan. Or do you want to wait to launch a business until you find a product or service that you can really get excited about. My suggestion? Don't start a business until you found one that you believe the world can't live without.

No assessment needed here—you know whether or not you've hit on an idea that keeps you up at night because you're so excited to bring it to the world. If you have, you can confidently go forward in this area of the assessment. But if you haven't, I suggest that you haven't yet found the right idea and you should put your launch plans on hold until you do.

One final word on this important trait in successful entrepreneurs. If you're on the fence, or don't know whether you have the passion to carry you through the hard times, I want you to ask yourself this important question: what would cause you to walk away? Be honest with yourself and make a list of everything that could possibly cause you to close the doors of your new business. Is it a lack of profit for a year or more? Write it down. The fact that you have no time for yourself or with your family? Make a note of it. After you've written down everything that could possibly cause you to walk away, you will know without a doubt whether or not you've hit on the right idea.

After all, most accomplished entrepreneurs will tell you that in order to build a successful business, it must be first in your life for a few years. If you can't make this particular idea first in your life for the foreseeable future, you're not on the right track.

A Willingness to Take Calculated Risks

There is no doubt that entrepreneurs are risk takers. After all, that's what separates them from the people who show up to work every day at someone else's business. They are willing to risk their money, time, job, career, and sometimes even their houses and individual finances.

But there are many people who are uncomfortable taking risks, and that typically doesn't go well for someone running their own business. People are generally scared of taking risks because of the following 2 reasons:

- **Fear that they can't handle the consequences.** Because we can never truly know whether a risk will succeed or fail, some people become so afraid of the potential consequences that they avoid risks altogether. And while that may work out (somewhat) in a personal life, it will never bear fruit while running a business. Entrepreneurs take risks every day. For example, when you hire someone, you're taking a risk on that person. When you release a new product or service, you're risking that it will be received well by the public. When you hang your shingle out, you're taking the risk that your business will succeed. In other words, if you can't take risks, you have no business running a business.
- **Expecting to fail.** Some people believe that no matter how hard they try, they are going to fail, so they end up never taking risks so that doesn't happen to them. But the truth is that if a risk is approached cautiously and with enough research, the chances of failure are reduced considerably.

"Calculated" is the Key Word

The one thing you won't find successful entrepreneurs doing is taking uncalculated risks.

Successful entrepreneurs only take calculated risks while the not-so-successful ones see risk taking as something that can be done glibly and based solely on gut or instincts. Unfortunately for them, they most often end up a statistic.

Let me give you an example. Imagine that your landscaping business is a year old, and you begin to think that adding pool services may help increase your profits. The person who is willing to take just any risk will purchase the expensive equipment, add the information to their website, create marketing tools such as brochures to give to their existing clients, spend advertising dollars trying to drum up new business for it, and maybe even hire some pool cleaning experts. They would do all of this without first understanding whether or not it is a good risk.

On the other hand, an entrepreneur who understands calculated risks would first survey their existing clientele to determine whether or not there is a need, conduct some research about how many pools are in the area, find out who is already doing it and what they charge for the service, estimate their equipment and labor costs to determine the potential profit, and then decide whether or not the move has the potential to grow their business.

Do you see the difference? Successful entrepreneurs only take risks based on research and planning, and that's why it's called calculated risks. We can never know the outcome of our risks, but if we first research and plan before deciding whether or not to take it, the odds of a successful outcome are increased.

The Assessment

When is the last time you took a risk? Whether it was in your personal life or in your job or business, I want you to think about the last time you took one and write down what the circumstances were. Was it asking for a promotion or raise? Deciding whether or not to buy a home? Or maybe you're facing a risk right now in deciding whether to leave your secure job and start your own business. Whatever risk you've faced in the past few months, think back to how you handled it. Did you approach it with confidence, do your homework, and then take the risk? Or did you go forward with only your gut instinct and bypass doing any kind of research or planning. Maybe you shied away from it, believing that you would fail—or couldn't possibly face the consequences—so you convinced yourself that you really didn't want to achieve the goal after all.

Your past actions are a pretty good indicator of your future behavior. But to get an even better idea of your risk taking tendencies, Testyourself.psychtests.com offers a great risk taking test that will show you which type of risk taker you are. Take the test, and then once you understand which type you are, use the next 30 days to refine your risk taking skills by using the following tips. Remember, learning how to take calculated risks will lead to successful business ventures.

Learn How to Take Calculated Risks

Now that you understand the importance of being adept at taking calculated risks, let's talk about how successful entrepreneurs do it. Here is a 4-step process that I'd like you to practice over the next 30 days.

- **Conduct research. A lot of it.** Whenever you're thinking about taking a risk, your first step should be to conduct as much research into the issue as possible. Just like in the pool cleaning example I used above, you should talk to anyone who has a clear understanding of the situation, research the competition, and run the numbers. Taking a risk should be based on knowledge and information, not a gut feeling.
- **Plan for the good and the bad.** Only a foolish risk taker would just focus on the possible good results and ignore the bad. As I said earlier, there is simply no way to determine whether or not a risk will pay off, but if you anticipate both the good and the bad, you'll be better equipped to decide if the risk is worth it—and be prepared for both outcomes. For example, the person deciding whether or not to add pool cleaning services to his landscaping business should think about the business-growing possibilities that could result from taking the risk, and also the bad. For instance, could the pool cleaning addition take too many resources from the landscaping arm of the business? If so, could the landscaping arm survive if the pool cleaning business takes 2 years to start turning a profit? If the pool cleaning arm of the business failed, how would the landscaping business respond to the loss of cash used to purchase all of the equipment?
- **Measure success in spurts.** When you take a risk, the payoff could come within a relatively short amount of time or it could take years. For example, people who start a business may not see the payoff for 2 years or more. That's why it's important to set milestones and checkpoints along the way—it helps stay focused on the main goal. For example, someone starting a new business may plan to become profitable within the first 8 months, and have a checkpoint set for

that time. This does 2 things for the risk taker. It helps keep them focused on the potential payoff of the risk so they don't lose motivation, and it also helps keep track of the risk's progress. For example, if the same person wasn't profitable by month 8, and only had financial resources to last 10 months, it would alert them to the possibility that they might need to change course. Which brings us to our next step...

- **Be flexible.** Things never go exactly as planned, even after you've done all the research and planning. That's part of what makes entrepreneurship so exciting—things rarely go exactly as you plan. But what you can control is your reaction to the changes. In the business world, it's called pivoting, and it means that when something doesn't go as planned, you pivot and change your course of action. For example, if the person we mentioned above realized that he may not become profitable before his 10 months of resources run out, he will have 2 choices. He can shrug his shoulders and give up, or he can pivot and go in a new direction. That may mean cutting more costs, eliminating the part of his new business that is draining the most funds without a good return, or try to find new capital. It would all depend on his numbers.

Of course, in the next 30 days, you won't be able to practice this method on anything but risks that involve short-term payoffs. But it's a start, and will help retrain your brain to view risks as the opportunities that they are. Keep a notebook and track your actions and the results and you'll soon see a pattern emerge.

A Refusal to Take No for an Answer

A good healthy belief in your product or service should produce in you a refusal to take no for an answer. History is full of people who refused to quit because they were told no time and time again. For example, the inventor of Miracle Mop, a woman who is worth about $40 million today, first began selling her mops locally. Then a TV shopping station bought 1,000 of them to sell themselves. She thought she'd hit on something big, but then when the mops failed to sell, the station asked her to take them back.

But she believed in her product, so she asked to go on TV and try to sell them herself. By the end of the broadcast, she'd sold about 180,000 mops.

Another great example of an entrepreneur who refused to take no for an answer is the creator of Airbnb. In the startup phase of his venture, the founder presented the idea to 7 potential investors and asked them for only $150,000. In exchange, he was willing to give them 10 percent of his business. Five of the investors rejected him outright and the other two never gave him an answer. Just imagine the world if he had allowed this rejection to cause him to give up on his dreams.

These are only 2 examples of entrepreneurs who refused to take no for an answer and went on to become huge successes in the business world. What do they have in common? An undying belief in their product or service.

We're not going to assess this trait, but I would like to refer you back to the section on Passion and Motivation. Remember, not having either of these will put your business at a greater risk of failure because you won't have that motivating factor that causes you to go forward, no matter what kind of obstacles you encounter.

As you can see, there are some pretty specific skills and traits that successful entrepreneurs share. The good news is that you can learn to use them all, provided that you put in the time and effort. The bad news is that if you don't take them seriously, the skill or trait that you don't take the time to develop could cause your business to fail.

What about you? Have you made note of your weaknesses and then followed the steps I've provided to help you overcome them? Please do so. If you're taking the time to read this book and assess your chances of success as a business owner, then you already understand the risks involved and know that you must do all you can to minimize them.

Once you've created a plan to overcome those weaknesses, it's time to move along and take a look at another important aspect of planning when starting a business: analyzing the product or service you plan to offer. Yes, it is possible to determine whether or not it will be a success before you launch it. Let's move on to the next chapter and I'll show you how.

Part Two: Do You Have a Product or Service That People Want to Buy? (How to Know and What to Do About It if You Don't.)

Having a product or service that people want to buy is of utmost importance when starting a business. There are many, many stories of entrepreneurs who had all the right skills, traits, and money to launch a business, but failed because there was simply no market for it.

Don't let this happen to you.

And while most books and mentors will tell you how important this is to the success of your business, they stop there. But I'm not going to leave you hanging. In this chapter, I lay out exactly how you can test your product or service to determine whether or not it will sell. And then I'll tell you what to do about it if it won't.

Here's the deal. Every single entrepreneur thinks his or her idea is the one that will set the world on fire. I don't care if you're planning on opening a neighborhood restaurant, plumbing business, accounting service, online store, book publishing business, or any other type of business, chances are that you think your business idea is better than all the others who came before you.

And that's okay because it takes that kind of passion and drive to succeed as a business owner.

But let's step outside of this for just a minute and look at some cold, hard facts.

CB Insights looked closely at 101 post-mortem essays (a post-mortem is an essay written by an entrepreneur after his or her business goes bust trying to explain why), and according to the company, 42 percent of those businesses failed because they tried to sell a product that no one wanted. In other words, there was no market for the product.

Does that make you sit up straighter and pay attention? It should, because although this isn't backed up by a poll or research, I think it's safe to say that those 42 percent were sure there was a market for their product or service. Otherwise, why would they have launched their business?

And that's why I think, after making sure you have the right personality traits and skills, this is the second most important area to look at when thinking about launching a business.

Now, let's talk about the many ways you can test your product or service before you launch it—all within the next 30 days.

Week 1: Start Small

If you're like most entrepreneurs, you want to start with a bang. You want to put your product or service out there and let the chips fall where they may. But slow down, because in order to get it right, you need to do some preliminary truth seeking first.

Remember the 42 percent of business owners who had to close their doors because they didn't first learn whether or not there was a market for their brilliant idea? If they had done the following steps they would have either abandoned their plans or continued to improve their product or service and saved themselves a lot of time, money, and frustration.

When testing the marketplace, it's best to start small. You want to start with a small circle in order to get some honest feedback, because this will determine whether you enlarge the size of your testing. Obviously, the larger the test, the more money it will cost, and that's why this first step is so crucial.

Your first step in the process should be to start with the people you know and trust, with one caveat: that they give you their honest opinion, no matter what. It won't help you if your family tells you that you have the best idea ever when they really think it's a dude. You need to be upfront with them and tell them that you're looking for an unbiased, honest opinion and ask them if they're capable of giving it to you. If they are, go forward.

How you go forward depends of what type of business you're planning. If you've invented a new product, you'll want to have this meeting before you spend the money to create a prototype of it. Simply explain the idea and ask for truthful feedback.

If you're starting a service business, talk to them about their perceived need for one in your town or city, and ask what they know about the competition. For example, can the area support another electrician or bookkeeper? Are there problems with the existing providers or do they have a loyal customer base?

And if you're thinking about opening a new restaurant, catering business, auto shop, house cleaning business, or other service business based on your skills alone, ask for honest feedback about your skills.

The same is true if you're considering opening an online store, or other type of business that will operate outside of your area such as a vending machine business. In this instance, you should ask those closest to you their opinion about how well you could run a business and get things done.

Remember, this is research, and you're asking for honest advice from those who know you the best. Don't get defensive and certainly don't brush off what you hear if it's not what you wanted them to say. Listen carefully and take everything in. If you hear something you didn't expect—like you should only cater events as long as you don't make the desserts, pay attention. Those criticisms and other truthful remarks could save your business.

Week 2: Go a Little Wider

If you feel confident about continuing your launch after you've met with friends and family, it's time to take your business idea to a group of neutral people who don't know you. Keep in mind that you can do this part of the process without first creating a prototype of any kind because you're still seeking information about the idea, not the product.

The reason I like to do this 1-2 punch instead of skipping to the actual product survey is because it acts as a buffer. You may or may not have received truly neutral feedback from your friends and family, or you may have discounted it as poor advice from your "Crazy Uncle Harry." But if you hear the same feedback from a completely neutral person, you will be more likely to listen to it.

The way you find these groups of neutral people will again depend on which type of business you plan to start. If your intended market is nationwide, such as an online business, or a business you plan to one day franchise across the nation, then you need to go online and create a focus group that is interested in your kind of business. Your goal for this type of "preliminary" focus group is to ask questions that give insight into what today's consumers want from a business like yours.

For example, if you want to open an online vintage clothing store, you will seek out buyers of vintage clothing and ask them if they believe there is room for another online store of this type, what existing stores are doing wrong or right, and what would cause them to give your store a try. Ask them about their thoughts about the competitor's pricing, shipping policies, return policies, and customer service. Ask about selection—what's currently offered and if there are any gaps or overages in it. In short, your goal is to find out what you will have to do differently or better in order to attract the vintage clothing crowd.

There are many online focus groups that you can use, but for this step, I recommend that you use a free service. You will conduct a more in-depth focus group later on and should expect to pay for that one, but for this step, you shouldn't have to spend any money. For example, FocusGroupit.com has a forever free plan that will allow you to form a focus group of up to 10 people. You can also set up your own Facebook focus group for free by following these steps:

- Go to the Home page on your Facebook page and look to the left. You'll see a listing of your groups, and under it an "add group" button. Click on it.
- On the next page, click on "Create New Group."
- You'll be asked to name your group. Choose a name that illustrates the group's purpose. For example, you may call it Landscaping Business Focus Group.

- Add your first member. Facebook won't allow you to create a group without adding at least 1 member, so add a friend to the group now.
- Set a privacy setting. You'll be able to choose between open, which means anyone can join in, closed, which only allows members to participate, but allows anyone else to see it, or secret, which is only visible to members. I recommend that you choose secret for a focus group.
- Click "Create."
- You'll then be given the option of displaying an icon for the group, and filling out the "about" section. The icon is a personal choice, but I would recommend filling out the about section to give future members a clear idea of the group's goal. You will also have the option of uploading a photo for the group.
- Make sure your settings are correct. For example, you may want to turn on notifications so that you are notified whenever someone from the group makes a comment or post.

On the other hand, if you plan to launch a local business, your focus group should be held in person. Your goal for a small, local focus group should be to ask many of the same questions that you did your family and friends, but these answers will come from people who have no skin in the game. They will be able to tell you about the local competition and what it would take for them to switch to your company. You should ask about what they want but aren't getting from existing stores or services and also about pricing and customer service.

To find participates for this small group, you can post an ad on Craigslist, put up a flyer in the local grocery store, post a message on your social media accounts, or just spread the word around your town.

How to Define Your Participants

Whether you're setting up a small preliminary focus group like this one, or a more detailed and comprehensive one like you will do later, you should define the desired characteristics of the participants before you put the word out. For example, in the scenario mentioned above, participants would be people who buy vintage clothing.

That's pretty simple and straightforward. But it can get more complex. If that vintage store focused on clothing made for young women, you might add an age requirement to the equation.

And if you're setting up a local focus group for a landscaping company, you may ask for people between the ages of 27 and 60 who own their own homes. The more specific your parameters are for the participants, the better information you'll receive.

Once you've conducted the focus group, be sure to compare the answers you received with the ones you heard from your friends and family. If you see a trend, pay special attention to it. For instance, if you hear from both groups that there is already too many businesses like yours, that's a red flag that your business may suffer from a lack of sales. On the other hand, if you hear that the current competitor lacks customer service, you'll know that having great customer service will set your business apart and you should focus on that area in your marketing efforts.

Week 3: It's Time to Test Your Product or Service

If you've made it through both focus groups with positive feedback, it's time to move on to the next step: testing your actual product or service with real people.

How you approach this task will depend on whether you want to open a local business or sell online, and also whether you will sell a product or service. Let's take a look at some of your options.

You Want to Sell a New Product

If you have created a new product, you'll need to test it on real consumers for a few reasons. First, and most importantly, you need to know whether a market for the product exists. Since there are no data to research—because the product doesn't exist yet—you will need to create a prototype of it and ask people to use it and report back to you.

Next, by creating a functional prototype, people will be able to use it and then give you feedback about what works, what doesn't, what could be better, and even which colors or styles are the most appealing. If the prototype has flaws, you can improve the model by creating a new one—and then test that. You may have to go through several variations of your product until you land on one that consumers like.

Eventually you will need to file for a patent for your new product, but it doesn't make sense to do that until you've perfected the model. If you file for a patent on your idea before you create a prototype, you may have to file for a new (and expensive) one if the design changes significantly after testing it.

Finally, if you plan to approach an angel investor or other type of lender, you will need to have a prototype of your product to show them so they can make a decision based on what the product looks like and how it performs.

For illustrative purposes, let's imagine that the garlic press has not yet been invented and you think it would make a hot new product. You've already spoken to the 2 focus groups and both have expressed an interest in the idea. They say it would help them save time in the kitchen, but of course, they would need to use one before giving you a final opinion. It's now time to create a prototype so they can do just that.

Here are the basic steps to creating a prototype of your new product:

- **Start by creating a homemade version of your prototype in an attempt to work out any bugs.** Doing this first will save you money because the most noticeable flaws will be spotted before you pay for the first professional prototype. You can use anything to build it—it doesn't have to be pretty—as long as it's functional and sturdy enough to test. If you're building a mechanical product, such as our garlic press, you can do it for about $15 by using a product called ShapeLock. This plastic melts in hot water so you can shape it, and then dries rigidly when subjected to room temperature. Test it yourself and then pass it around to people you know. Ask for opinions about flaws and improvements and keep creating new homemade prototypes until you feel the product is perfect.
- **Have a computer-aided design (CAD) made.** Next, you'll need to hire an engineer to create a CAD. You should expect to pay about $125 an hour for the service.

- **Now it's time to approach a professional to ask for a prototype.**
  Depending on your budget, you can either ask the local carpenter, a mold shop, an industrial design student at the local university, someone with a 3D printer, or a machinist to design the prototype for you. If you're not that limited in your finances, there are plenty of prototype designers you can work with. The best way to find them is to go to Thomasnet.com. There, you'll find a huge list of prototype engineers to choose from. The cost can vary wildly, depending on the design and whether or not any electronics are involved. You'll want to look for someone who provides rapid prototyping based on your CAD because the cost is much less than the standard injection mold process. For example, you could pay as little as $300 for this less expensive version compared to thousands of dollars for the traditional process.

Once you have your prototype made, it's time to test it again with consumers. Keep testing the product until you stop hearing about flaws and possible improvements. Once you've reached a point where you feel that the prototype is the best it can be, it's time to set up another focus group. We'll talk about how to set it up in detail after the next section.

You Want to Open a Local Service Business

Maybe you don't want to invent a new product, but want to use your skills to open a service business. You could open a house cleaning business, bookkeeping service, barber shop or beauty salon, cottage food business, lawn mowing service, or another type of business where you can use your skills.

Unlike a product-based business, a service business is built upon your skills, and just as with a new product, you will need to test those skills on consumers to get constructive feedback.

For instance, if you want to open a housekeeping business, you will need to set up some free cleanings for neutral parties and then ask for feedback. For example, you can post the offer at your kid's school, on a local forum, your social media accounts, or ask friends for recommendations. The key is to find people who don't know you and can be neutral in their evaluation of your services.

You'll need to set up a few free cleanings (Or haircuts, tattoos, meal preparation, yard work, or whatever service you're offering) and ask for written feedback from each one of them. Make it clear that you're looking for constructive criticism and ask them to tell you what they liked and didn't like, what you could do better, and whether or not they believe you can make it in business.

It's important to deliver the exact type of service that you'll later charge people for. For example, if you plan to offer light housekeeping, don't deep clean the person's house. Instead, explain to them that you will only offer light housekeeping and ask them to rate you on that. If you plan to open a farmer's market booth selling baked goods, bake the exact same items you plan to sell in your booth and get feedback on them. Did they like it? Would they buy it again? Could it be improved in any way?

Now, take your notes from each of your tests and compare them. Are there any patterns or trends, either positive or negative? If so, identify them and figure out how to incorporate the feedback and make your product or service better.

Week 4: The Final Focus Group

Once you've reached this point, you have a pretty clear picture of what people like and don't like about your product or service. You've heard the good and the bad, and hopefully you've made adjustments based on that.

Now it's time to take the finished product or service to one last focus group and get as much information as you can.

Because this will be the last step in your product testing, you will need to put a lot more time and effort into creating it. In short, you're going to try and get as much information as you can from the group, and use it to increase your chances of a successful launch.

Here is how you should set up this important group:

- **If you're selling a product nationwide, choose between an online group or an in-person group.** I recommend that you do it in person because it's easier to interact with the group that way. If you're selling a local product or service, you will have to create a local focus group.
- **Choose the location.** You should strive to select a location that's convenient to everyone. If you're located in a small town, it should be easy but if you're located in a larger city, try to pick a location that is central to most people. Make sure there is ample parking nearby and make it easy for people to find by sending out clear directions.
- **Decide on a payment method.** Most focus groups pay the participants a fee for their efforts. These fees typically range from $50 to $200 and you can find willing participants in every price range. As a business owner, you will need to decide the payment based on your budget. Focus groups typically last between 1-2 hours.
- **Hire a moderator.** As tempting as it is to oversee the focus group yourself, don't do it. An experienced moderator knows how to ask the questions in a way that produces the most productive and informative answers. He or she will also be able to keep the conversation on track and coax additional information from participants so you can get the most out of the time. An experienced moderator can help you devise the best questions, find the right participants, and then analyze the data afterwards. To find a good, local moderator, conduct a search at QRCA.org or the directory at Quirks.com.
- **Create the questions.** You have to go into the focus group prepared, and that means you need to know in advance what questions you plan to ask the participants. Most focus groups are asked between 5-7 questions, and because there will be a lot of interaction between the participants, you should plan on spending about 2 hours there. Devise your questions by determining what you need to know to make your business a success. Ask about the product or service first—they will have the prototype, or you will have performed the service for them—and then get into other things such as what could make your business stand out from competitors, what they consider a fair price for it, and what would

cause them to become a repeat customer. Remember, your moderator will help you devise the questions, but he or she will rely on your industry expertise to do so.

- **Find the participants.** You will need to narrow down the characteristics of your participants as much as possible to get the most out of the session. For example, if you were forming a focus group for the house cleaning business, you might want to look for working women in affluent neighborhoods, or single moms who own their own home. You can advertise for them on social media or Facebook groups, and if you offer referral bonuses, your group will quickly grow. Limit it to 10 people, otherwise it could get unruly. Remember, a good moderator will help you determine these guidelines and then help find the participants.
- **Record the session.** Instead of trying to remember everything each participant said, it's smart to simply record the session. Be sure to inform everyone that it is being recorded.

Once you've set up the focus group, it's time to sit back and let the moderator handle it professionally. While you'll likely want to jump in and talk about the virtues of your product or service, don't. The moderator is a neutral party and will best be able to get the most helpful information from the participants.

If, after this last focus group, you're getting positive feedback, you should feel confident in going forward with your idea. The plan I've outlined in this chapter is almost foolproof. And according to the research I shared with you earlier, it's probably a lot more than the 50 percent of failed business owners did.

Isn't it amazing? In 30 days, you've have a clear idea about whether or not the product or service you want to launch will resonate with consumers. But before we go to the next chapter, we need to address one more thing.

What to Do if People Don't Like Your Product or Service

If you find yourself reading this section because you've received negative feedback about your product or service, I'm sorry. I'm not known to beat around the bush, so I'm just going to talk turkey with you for a moment, okay?

There is a reason that I've asked you to test your product or service before you launch your business. So many entrepreneurs make the mistake of thinking that they know best when it comes to what people want and they ignore all of the warning signs. Unfortunately, it's those business owners who have to close up shop.

If people weren't receptive to your new product idea, it means the time hasn't yet come. It may be a popular idea 5 years from now, or it may never be. And if you received negative feedback on your service, it may not be right business model for you either.

Here's what I know. If you want to start a business, you can. But it has to be the *right* one in order for it to succeed. You're reading this book because you want to ensure that your business will succeed, and the testing you just did shows that it probably won't.

So what are you going to do?

Will you forge ahead anyway and likely end up a statistic? Or will you accept that you haven't yet hit on the right idea and keep looking? I want you to succeed, I really do, and based on my experience, I can tell you unequivocally that if your product or service idea did not do well in the testing stage, it won't fly. I'm sorry, but that's just the truth.

So what do you do?

You keep looking. Just because this idea wasn't the right one, that doesn't mean you don't have the right idea in you. Keep looking, and when you think you've hit on another idea, conduct the same tests. And when you find one that people love, continue on to the next chapter.

Remember, your dreams are your own, but when it comes to starting a business, you must have a product or service that people are willing to pay for. Anything else is just an expensive hobby.

The Next Step

Okay, so you've analyzed and improved your personality traits and skills, you've tested, tested, and tested again your product or service idea, and now it's time to talk about finances. Are you financially able to start your own business? Let's find out in the next chapter.

Part Three: Do You Have Enough Money to Start This Business? (How to Know and What to Do About it if You Don't.)

It's time to talk about the role of finances in your new business—and I hope you have a nice cup of tea or coffee at your side because it's going to be a long one. This is the chapter that many of you will be tempted to skip because we're going to talk about "boring" numbers, formulas, and budgets, but I'm asking you forge on.

Reading and understanding this chapter will play a significant role in whether or not you are successful in your small business launch.

I've become disturbed lately by all the eBooks and blog posts that I've read telling would-be entrepreneurs that they don't really need a business plan or that they don't have to make financial projections before starting a business.

Please sit up and read this carefully. Yes. You. Do.

Sure, many people start a business without first understanding the financial implications or how to properly manage their cash flow, but chances are, they are in the 50 percent of business owners who fail.

Listen to me—if you want to launch a business that will be successful, provide you with a great income, and allow you to have financial freedom, you must do some math before you launch.

It's simply not an option.

A financial blueprint will give you a roadmap that allows you to set goals, understand how and when milestones should be reached, calculate the usefulness of future expenditures, and give you a grasp of your business' health at all times.

In other words, it's like a GPS system for your business. Without it, you're just going to get lost.

So, let's take apart this big topic step by step. I'm not only going to outline what you need to do to get your financial life in order so you can start a business, I'm going to give you detailed instructions on how to do it.

I want to concentrate on the four main areas of finance that will show you whether or not you are ready to launch your business. (One for each week in our 30-day challenge) First, we'll talk about the amount of money you will need to open your doors, then we'll talk about how much money you can expect to earn in the first year. Next, I'll show you how to calculate your break-even point—that point when your business finally begins to turn a profit. And finally, we'll talk about those long-range goals I mentioned in the last chapter.

Are you ready? Let's first talk about how to know how much money you will need to start your business, and how to make sure that you don't fall short.

Step One: Analyze Your Expenses

Your first step in understanding your financial landscape is to get a picture of all your monthly expenses, both personal and business. Remember, you will no longer have a regular income from your full-time job, so you'll need to have enough money to pay for your living expenses for a set amount of time.

It's a common misunderstanding to think that the business will pay your expenses in the beginning—it will take you some time to ramp up and begin earning enough profits to pay the bills. Besides, the money that comes into your business in the beginning should be put back into it in order to grow it.

Instead, you'll need to go into the business with 6-12 months of expenses in your pocket. I highly recommend that you begin with 12 months of expenses, because if you run out before you turn a profit, like the business owner in our example in the last chapter, your business will be at risk of closure.

Week 1: How Much Money Will it Take to Open Your Doors?

This is a crucial part of the equation, and one that many new entrepreneurs get wrong. Human tendency seems to underestimate things when we're counting the costs for doing something we really want to. And that's why so many new businesses run out of money and have to close the doors. I urge you to be real in these calculations, because if you underestimate and run out of money halfway through your first year, it could be the end of your dreams.

Let's first talk about how much money you'll need to pay your personal bills.

Calculate Your Personal Expenses

Let's start by looking at what you need to earn every month at a minimum for your personal expenses. Please add up these expenses:

- Mortgage/rent
- Homeowners/renters insurance
- Utilities
- Car payments
- Car insurance
- Food
- Debt payments
- Monthly subscriptions
- Eating out expenses *I recommend eliminating all non-necessary expenses the first year of your business.
- Gas
- Phone
- Internet
- Clothing *Most people have a full wardrobe, and if you do, I also recommend living with the clothes you already have until your business begins to turn a profit.
- Savings/retirement
- Emergency fund
- Any other unique expenses you have that you pay every month

Add up all of these expenses, and multiply it by 12. For example, if your living expenses total $2,500 a month, you will need to have at least $30,000 in living expenses saved up before you're ready to open your business.

Calculate Your Business Expenses

But wait, in addition to your personal expenses, you'll also have to pay the bills for your business. Here's where it gets a little tricky because you don't yet know exactly what those bills will be, but I'm going to show you how to create a pretty good estimate with some research.

Here are some of the monthly expenses you may incur, depending on which type of business you plan to open.

- Rent. (You may not have this expense if you operate a home-based business.)
- Utilities
- Car or truck payment. (If you run a service business, you may or may not need to purchase a specialized vehicle.)
- Gas
- Payroll service *optional
- Taxes (The Tax Cut and Jobs Act, which takes effect in 2018, allows pass through companies (Sole-proprietor, S-corporation, LLC, or LLP) to deduct the first 20 percent of profits from their tax bill—as long as it's less than $315,000 for married filers, and $157,500 for single filers. That means if you make $100,000 in adjusted gross income, you will only pay taxes on $80,000 of it.) Taxfoundation.org has a [marginal tax rate chart](#) you can use to estimate your taxes. (We'll estimate those first year profits later in this chapter.)
- Accounting software (Or you use a free service like Mint.com)
- Phone
- Internet *(f you work from home, you may be able to use your personal internet connection, and even your own phone.)

You will have to do some research-based guestimates on these expenses, but it shouldn't be too difficult. For example, if you plan to rent an office space or storefront, contact a Realtor and ask about rent prices in the area you want to locate your business in. If you'll need to purchase a car or truck, talk to a dealership and get some ball park figures. The same is true for accounting software, and phone and internet fees—those rates are easily found online for your area.

I want to stress something here—your goal is to have the least amount of monthly expenses as possible because that will give your business the best chances for success. If you already have a truck you can use, don't go buy a new one until your business' profits can justify it. And if you have to answer your personal phone with your business name for a while, so be it. Start small and grow from there.

Now, add up your estimated monthly business expenses and multiply it by 12. For instance, if you're planning to work from home and can get by with $500 in expenses, you should multiply that by 12 and come to $6,000 in business expenses for the year.

Add that to the $30,000 in personal expenses, and you will need $36,000 for expenses in the first year of your business.

But wait, we're not finished.

Calculate Your Startup Costs

You also need to calculate your startup expenses, because that's the money you will need to spend before you open your doors. Again, this figure will be based on informed guesses.

Here's a list of some possible startup expenses you'll need to figure in:

- Logo design
- Website design and creation
- Printed marketing materials such as brochures, business cards, and signage
- Improvements to a retail location or addition to your home for an office
- Attorney's fee or legal work

- Specialized software
- Specialized equipment
- Office supplies
- Deposits

These are just some of the startup costs that you may incur, and depending on your type of business, there could be many more. You'll need to think carefully about what you will need for your unique business to open its doors and then include it in this list.

There are some great free startup cost worksheets available online. For example, the SBA offers a startup cost worksheet in PDF form as does QuickBooks.

Again, call around and get prices and come up with as realistic of an estimate as you can. Once you have a good number, add it to your running total. For example, if you estimate your startup costs to be $10,000, your new total is $46,000.

At this point, you'll need to make some decisions about how you will get the money to start your business. You'll have 3 choices: 1) keep your day job and bootstrap the business, 2) use money you already have in savings, and 3) borrow the money. Let's talk about each of these below.

How to Bootstrap Your Business

Taking on as little debt as possible when starting a business is smart. It reduces your monthly expenses and allows you to put more money back into growing your business. Moonlighting is the ideal way to bootstrap your business, and we'll start out by taking about that. Then, I'll offer a few more ideas to help you start out with less debt.

Keep Your Day Job

Depending on what type of job you have, it may be smart to keep it and use your salary to help finance your new business. In recent years, this has become known as the side hustle. And while that's a catchy word, the truth is that people have always used "moonlighting" to earn extra income by starting a new business on the side.

If this sounds like an option to you, here are some things you should consider when making your decision:

- **Think about your salary.** If you're earning a six-figure salary, it make sense to start your business as a side hustle because that big salary could help support the business, in addition to paying your personal bills. But if you work in a low-income job, it may not make sense. After all, low paying jobs barely cover living expenses, and it will limit the amount of time you have to grow your new business.
- **Think about time constraints.** Some businesses take more time than others to run, or won't allow for after hours working schedules. For example, if you're thinking about opening a professional service, clients will expect you to be available during work hours. On the other hand, if you're opening a freelance writing business, you'll be able to work anytime of the day for most projects and should have no problem operating it as a side hustle.
- **What about insurance?** If you have a large family and have health care through your employer, you might consider running your business as a side hustle until it turns enough of a profit to allow you to purchase health insurance on your own.
- **Would it be a breach of ethics?** Finally, if you're starting a business that would be in direct competition with the company you currently work for, you could be walking a fine line by continuing to work there. And that could lead to disagreements, lawsuits, and even a ruined reputation for your business. Read your employee agreement to find out if your employer has any rules on moonlighting. For example, some tech companies lay claim to the intellectual property rights of anything you create in your off time. Other agreements prohibit you from running a side-hustle.

Other Ways to Bootstrap Your Business

Here are some other ways you can use bootstrapping to reduce the amount of startup capital you'll need:

- **Ask for trade credit.** When a new business first opens, most manufacturers will set up COD terms until it can prove that it will pay its bills on time. But if you present a manufacturer with a written financial plan and negotiate with them, you may persuade them to extend you credit. This will allow you keep the money for cost of goods about 30 days longer, which will help jumpstart your business.
- **Buy expensive equipment on terms.** If you plan to open a business that requires expensive equipment, you could save a lot of upfront capital expenses by asking the manufacturer to sell you the equipment via a loan. There are 2 common types of agreements. 1) a sales contract where you would not officially own the equipment until it's paid. This is similar to a car loan, or 2) a chattel-mortgage contract. In this scenario, you own the equipment, but the manufacturer holds a mortgage on it until the note is paid in full.
- **Lease high-ticket items.** Another way to bootstrap your business is to lease high-ticket items instead of paying cash for them upfront. For example, if you need office equipment, you can lease it for a small monthly payment instead of shelling out thousands for it upfront. The same is true for a service truck or other cash-depleting items. If you decide to go this route, it will up your monthly expenses, so be sure to run the numbers first to make sure it's a good move for you. And if you decide to go this route, you should purchase the item outright as soon as your business begins turning a profit in order to reduce your overhead.

Use Your Savings to Start a Business

If you have savings in the bank, it may be wise to use that money as your startup capital. In fact, 77 percent of entrepreneurs used some or all of their savings to start their business. However, if you do, so you keep the following in mind:

- **Don't deplete your entire account.** Make sure you keep an emergency fund in your savings for the unexpected. Most experts agree that your emergency fund should contain a minimum of 3 months of living expenses. You just never know when your car will break down or something else will happen and you'll need instant access to money.

- **Use your savings as leverage for a low-interest loan.** Another option you have is to keep your savings intact, and then use it as collateral for a low-interest loan from friends and family. This will ensure that you have the capital if the unexpected happens and you need additional funds for your business. For example, you may receive a large order, and need the money in order to fulfill it.
- **Use your 401(k).** I'll talk about this in detail in the next section, but it is possible to use your 401(k) or other retirement account to finance your business.

How to Find a Loan to Finance Your Business

Finally, sometimes you'll need to look to lenders to find startup capital, and luckily, today's entrepreneurs have a lot of choices. Here are some of the ways you can find startup capital via loans:

Borrow from Friends and Family

I see a lot of experts warn people about borrowing small business capital from friends or family because they say it could potentially harm their relationships. I take a different approach. As long as you treat the transaction like a business deal—and stick to what you promise—I see no reason why this can't be a viable and important way to get startup capital. After all, Jeff Bezos not only started Amazon.com in his garage, but he borrowed money from his parents to do it. In fact, 82 percent of new business owners got their startup capital from friends and family.

If you're going to take this small business startup loan option, be sure to follow these guidelines.

- **Approach them like a business person.** When you approach a bank for a business loan, you prepare and present your business idea to them in a way that allows them to analyze it before making a funding decision. It should be no different with your friends and family. Present them with your research and business plan just as you would any other investor. This will not only gain their respect, but it will give them all the information they need to make an intelligent decision based on the facts.

- **Don't pressure them into a decision.** Rather than asking them to make a decision on the spot, tell them that you will leave the information with them so they can think about it. Whether you succeed or fail in your venture, you want your investors to own the decision they made, and if you pressure them into a "yes," that could cause them to harbor resentment towards you if you fail.
- **Make it legal.** Whatever you do, don't come to an agreement on a handshake. You will need to draw up legal documents just like you would if you were borrowing from a bank or other investor. This will prevent misunderstandings from occurring in the future, which could put a damper on your relationship.
- **Keep your word.** Finally, whatever terms you agree to, it's imperative that you keep up your end of the bargain. If you promise them a percentage of the profits, you'll need to provide them with financial reports on a regular basis to show what the company is earning. If you agree to a payback schedule, make it priority to never miss a deadline. And if you get into financial trouble, be sure to talk to them about it immediately instead of avoiding them.

Use Credit Cards to Fund a Small Business Startup

One small business financing option you have is to use your personal credit card to fund your business. It's estimated that about half of the startups in the US use credit cards to finance their business. Using credit cards to fund a new startup is fast and you won't have to jump through a lot of hoops to use them, but although this method of funding a business is readily available to many, it doesn't come without risks.

For starters, if your business fails or you are unable to meet the minimum monthly payments on the credit card, your personal credit will be at risk. And while it would be better to get and use a business credit card, chances are you won't be able to when just starting out because your business won't have a credit history. To change this, you can apply to vendors such as office supply stores and then build your business credit from there.

Another risk with using credit cards to fund a small business is that those minimum monthly payments can add up quickly if the interest rate is too high. For example, if you financed $20,000 on a credit card that charged 23 percent interest, your monthly payment would be about $583.00. That's a big chuck of change when trying to get a new business off the ground.

Many people have achieved success by using credit cards to fund a business, but they approached the funding method cautiously and carefully. If you're thinking about using this option to fund your new business, be smart and let the credit cards work for you, not the other way around.

Use a 401K or Other Retirement Plan for a Small Business Startup

If you have money in a 401K, 403(b), SEP, TSP, or Keogh you may be able to use it to fund your business. But be warned, if you decide to go this route and your business fails, you will not only lose your business, but your retirement savings as well.

The IRS has a special plan called ROBS (Rollover for Business Startups) that allows entrepreneurs to use their 401K retirement plan for a business startup. If you meet these requirements, you may be able to use your retirement funds to finance your small business.

- **You must own the retirement account.** If your 401K or other retirement plan is set up by your employer and they control it, you cannot use it to fund your startup. This only works if you have an individual account, or if you've recently left your job but still have the account.
- **Only certain types of retirement plans are eligible**. Your money must be in one of the types of retirement accounts listed above to be eligible. If you have retirement funds in another type of account, consider converting it into one of the eligible types.
- **You will not have to pay fees**. If you're not yet 59 1/2, and withdraw funds from your retirement account, you will have to pay income taxes on the money you withdraw, as well as a 10 percent penalty. But if you're using the ROBS program, those fees are waved. In addition, because this is not a loan, you won't have to burden your new business with interest payments.

There are some very specific steps you'll need to follow to stay on the good side of the IRS when using this program, and I recommend that if you plan to use your 401K to finance a startup, you meet with a financial planner to get it right.

- **Your new business must be set up as a C corporation.** Because different states have various law on how to do this, you may need to hire a lawyer to do it right. Once set up this way, you'll need to designate a board of directors, officers, shareholders, resident agent, and file articles of incorporation.
- **Open a 401K plan for your business.** Make sure the business 401K plan you open has a profit sharing plan that allows 100 percent of the assets attributable to rollovers to be invested in employee stock.
- **Make the transfer.** Transfer the funds from your personal 401K to the business 401K and then invest it in your company's stock.

Some experts say that using retirement accounts for small business startups increase the likelihood of an IRS audit, so make sure that if you use this funding method, you do it correctly.

Get a Bank Loan for a Small Business Startup

Even though bank loans have become more and more scarce for small business owners because banks have tightened the lending process considerably, there are still instances when a bank loan may make sense. For example, if you have a perfect credit score, a well-thought out and persuasive business plan and at least 30 percent of the loan amount as collateral, a bank may give you a second look.

And some types of banks are beginning to loosen their purse strings in order to provide small business loans to entrepreneurs. For instance, credit unions are said to be making small loans at twice the rate of large banks.

If you think you could qualify for a bank small business loan, this should be your first step because the interest rates and fees are considerably lower than other lending sources. But plan ahead if this is your first choice because the wait times are longer than the newer, alternative forms of startup funding.

Use SBA Startup Loans to Fund Your Business

The Small Business Administration (SBA) itself doesn't lend money to anyone, but it partners with traditional banks and micro lenders to lend money to entrepreneurs looking for new business loans. The rates are typically lower than most traditional bank loans because the SBA guarantees a portion of them, so the banks know that at least some of the loan will be repaid even if the business goes under.

These loans are great for people who can't quite qualify for a traditional bank loan, but still want lower interest rates and repayment terms. In order to qualify for a traditional SBA startup loan, you must have good credit (a credit score of at least 720), some collateral, and some business experience. SBA micro loans are for those who don't have stellar credit. The SBA offers a state-by-state list of approved micro loan lenders on their website.

Here are a few facts about SBA loans:

- SBA offers micro loans with a cap of $50,000.
- SBA offers its signature 7(a) loan for startups that have a little more experience and better credit. They typically range from about $500 to over $5 million.
- APRs start at 6.5 percent and go up, depending on the credit history of the borrower.
- It can take 3 weeks to a few months to apply for and get an SBA loan.
- Repayment terms are typically 10 years, but can range from 5 to 25 years.

Get a Microloans for a Small Business Startup

The SBA isn't the only organization offering microloans for small business startups. You can find these easier-to-quality-for loans from a variety of sources.

Microloans are easier to qualify for, and are intended for people who need a small amount of startup cash (Typically under $50,000). While you still need an acceptable credit score, you won't need perfect credit to be approved. And although you will still need to submit some basic documents such as a business plan, the requirement aren't as stringent as traditional bank loans. Depending on your credit history, you may be asked to provide collateral, or if you don't have any, a personal guarantee for the loan amount.

Microloan lenders tend to look at your potential rather than your experience, and that makes these loans particularly good for entrepreneurs in the startup phase. Some of the places that offer microloans are Kabbage.com, Lending Club.com, and Prosper.com. Both Lending Club and Prosper are peer to peer lending, which means investors will look at your proposal and decide if they want to fund a portion of your business. Kabbage is a direct lender.

Use Crowdfunding and Equity Lending for Small Business Startup Funds

A creative business owner can go to sites like KickStarter.com and Indiegogo.com and ask for funding in the form of gifts. For example, someone wanting to write a book could describe the project, ask for donations, and then give donors gifts such as a signed copy of the book or a lunch with the author. This is still a great way to raise startup capital for a creative business. Because the money is donated in exchange for gifts, there is no repayment and that's a major benefit for any new business owner.

But in 2013, the JOBS Act was signed into law, and it changed the playing field. The new law allowed entrepreneurs to seek investment funds from accredited investors on crowdfunding sites. The accredited investors must have earned $200,000 in the past 2 years or have $1 million in net worth, apart from their primary residence.

Then, in 2016 the law was expanded and now anyone can invest in startup companies. People whose net worth is less than $100,000 can invest a maximum of $2,000 or up to 5 percent of their net worth or annual income, whichever is less. And those making more than that can invest 10 percent of their net worth or annual income, whichever is less.

This has opened up startup capital funding for entrepreneurs all over the country because they no longer have to go to a bank or other lender, but can pitch their business idea directory to investors.

Sites like Crowdfunder.com, equity.indiegogo.com, and Wefunder.com allow everyday people to invest in startups. If you have a business idea that will appeal to the masses, this may be the startup funding option for you.

As you can see, these options may or may not be available to you, depending on your credit history. I'd like to talk to you about both your personal and business credit history, because frankly, until you have them under control, you're not ready to start a business.

Get Your Credit Score Up to Standards

Let's start by looking at why your personal and business credit history is so important.

- Because your business is in the startup stages, many lenders will ask you to sign personally for a loan. You can't do this unless your personal credit history is good.
- You will have a difficult time finding a small business loan without a good credit score. In fact, 45 percent of would-be borrowers are turned down because of their credit scores.
- Your business credit score isn't private. Potential creditors, suppliers, customers, and anyone else can see it, and if it's not good, it will directly affect your credibility.
- If you do manage to find a small business loan with bad credit, you'll pay a much higher interest rate, which means your profits will be slashed. In addition, that higher interest rate will only add to your monthly expenses because it will make the payment higher.

Can you see why building a good credit score is so important? If yours isn't what it should be, here are some tips for improving it.

- **Maintain your scores.** There are 3 credit agencies that keep track of business credit scores and you should maintain all 3 because you never know which one your creditors will check. They are 1) Dun & Bradstreet, 2) Experian, and 3) Equifax. Each one rates business credit scores differently, so it's important to stay on top of all 3 to ensure your business is being represented fairly.
- **Set up trade lines as soon as possible.** We talked about asking manufacturers to extend trade credit before to help bootstrap your business, but it's also important to help build a good credit score. For example, Dun & Bradstreet won't even give you a credit score until you have 3 trade lines. If you have problems convincing a manufacturer to take a chance on your new business, start with an office supply store or some other smaller trade credit and build from there. If the suppliers don't report to the credit agencies, Dun & Bradstreet will follow up with those you list.
- **Pay your invoices early.** Some credit agencies, such as Dun & Bradstreet give you extra points on your credit score if you pay your suppliers early. In fact, the agency only hands out perfect credit scores to those businesses that do. Pay your invoices early to improve your credit score.
- **Stay in the clear legally.** In addition to your payment history, business credit reports show any liens, bankruptcies, and judgements, so make sure your record stays clean. Remember, potential customers and suppliers will read your report.

Wow, that was a busy week wasn't it? But getting your finances in order to start a business is vital to the success of your business. Let's move on to week 2 where we'll learn how to estimate the profits you can expect to make in the first year.

Week 2: Estimate Your First Year Profits

Now that you understand just how much money it will take to open your doors, let's spend a little time learning how to estimate your first year profits. While this step also involves some guessing, it's critical to your planning stages. After all, what if you found out that you needed to spend $46,000 to start but could only expect a profit of $5,000 in the first year. Hopefully that would cause you to rethink your move.

Keep in mind that sales forecasting is a series of strategic guesses, meaning that no human being has the ability to predict the future. But with some research and logic based assumptions, you should be able to get close.

Your sales forecast is a living document and it's meant to be changed as your assumptions and facts change. So don't worry about making a mistake in the beginning or trying to get it exact. The exercise is supposed to reflect your assumptions of what your first year will bring, and those assumptions will change over time.

Here's how to create your first year's sales projections.

To begin, you'll need to look for sales drivers. For example, our landscaping and pool guy could count the number of houses that have a pool in his target area and make an assumption that he will get 50 percent of the business. His assumption is based on the fact that his competitor is known for not returning calls or doing a poor job. Or you may want to open a restaurant. In that case, you should design your floorplan to determine how many tables and chairs it will hold, and then visit your competitors during different times of the day to learn how many tables they serve every hour.

Again, it's not a science, but if you make the right assumptions backed by observations and research, you'll be surprised at how close you can get.

Remember too that most industries have seasons, and that should be reflected in your assumptions. For instance, our pool guy will show much higher sales number in the summer than the winter.

This exercise will be easier if you know your industry because you'll already understand the ups and downs of the business. For example, if you work in the pool cleaning business and are about to start your own pool business, you will know how many pools a day you currently service and which months are busier than others.

If you are stuck and can't make assumptions that you're comfortable with, it's okay to reach out to someone and ask for help. You could call a similar business in another city and ask them for some guidance, or you could call SCORE and set up a meeting with a free mentor who will help walk you through the process.

But remember, you can do this. It only takes some basic research and a willingness to make some assumptions based on what you learn and observe.

After you've made those assumptions, make an educated guess about your projected sales goals for each month of the year and enter them into a spreadsheet.

Next, we'll need to figure your costs in order to get to our gross profit figure.

To do that, you need to determine your cost per unit. This depends on what type of business you're operating. For example, if you sell hats and pay $2 each for them, that's your cost per unit. But if you run a service business, your cost per unit is the cost of doing business, such as gas or salaries, and you'll need to estimate that per job.

Once you arrive at your cost per unit, multiply it by the number of units you project you will sell in each month. That's how much it costs you to sell those units.

For each month of the year, you should have your estimated number of sales, the sales figure (number of sales x retail price), the cost per unit price, and total costs (number of sales x cost per unit). Then deduct the total costs from the total sales and you'll have an estimate gross profit for every month of the next year. Your figures might look something like this:

	A	B	C	D
16	**Sales Forecast**			
17			Jan	Feb
18	**Unit Sales**			
19	Widgets	30%	187	144
20	Whatsits	40%	374	288
21	Other	10%	56	43
22	**Total Unit Sales**		617	475
23				
24	**Unit Prices**		Jan	Feb
25	Widgets		$25.00	$25.00
26	Whatsits		$50.00	$50.00
27	Other		$10.00	$10.00
28				
29	**Sales**			
30	Widgets		$4,675	$3,600
31	Whatsits		$18,700	$14,400
32	Other		$560	$430
33	**Total Sales**		$23,935	$18,430
34				
35	**Direct Unit Costs**		Jan	Feb
36	Widgets	25.00%	$6.25	$6.25
37	Whatsits	35.00%	$17.50	$17.50
38	Other	40.00%	$4.00	$4.00
39				
40	**Direct Cost of Sales**			
41	Widgets		$1,169	$900
42	Whatsits		$6,545	$5,040
43	Other		$224	$172
44	**Subtotal Direct Cost of Sales**		$7,938	$6,112

Remember, you're not trying to predict the future with your projections. You are simply putting your assumptions on paper so you can track them as the year goes on. This will allow you to see your business growth from a logical point of view and make changes as you see necessary. For example, if you're not reaching your sales projections, you may decide to increase your marketing efforts. Or if your price per unit cost changes, it may cause you to look for another supplier or increase your sales price. Think of your sales projections as a guide that will help you make better decisions as you run your business.

But for now, think of it as a reference for whether or not your business idea is a profitable one. Do you see enough profits in the first year to make the venture worthwhile for you? Do you need to add more products or services to make the business viable?

If your projected profits aren't what you thought they would be, then it's either time to rethink your decision about launching this business, or pivot and change up your idea. But if the numbers are in your favor, then you've likely hit on the right idea.

Now, let's talk about when your business may start to turn a profit.

Week 3: Figure Your Break-even Number

No business is profitable in the early stages, but every company has a break-even point—that magical moment when it starts to be profitable. And of course, every business is different and will reach that point at various times.

But luckily, there is a calculation that you can use to guestimate your break-even point. And that is important for many reasons. For starters, it will show you how long you will need to work at the business before expecting to earn a profit. Once a business becomes profitable, things become easier because it will be able to pay some (or all) of its expenses, your salary, and may even allow you to hire an employee or two.

Let's talk about how to calculate the break-even point for your business.

For this calculation, you'll need 3 figures, all derived from the above exercises. You'll need your projected monthly sales, your cost per unit price, and your monthly business expenses.

The calculation looks like this:

Break-even point = fixed costs / (average price per unit – average cost per unit)

To illustrate this, let's imagine that our fixed costs are $2,500 a month, our average price per unit is $100, and our average cost per unit is $30.

We subtract $30 from $100 to arrive at $70. Then we divide $70 into $2,500 and learn that we have to sell 29 units per month in order to break even. Anything that we sell over that is profit.

Now, take that figure and look at your sales projections. Look for the month when your projections say that you will sell the required number of units to break even and mark it as a milestone. If all goes according to plan, that's the month that your business will begin to earn a profit.

You can also use this figure to tweak your business assumptions. For example, if you want to break even earlier, you can up your retail price and that would mean you would have to sell less units to become profitable.

Can you see how useful this type of information is when deciding whether or not to start your business now or later? Think about it for a minute. Of all those entrepreneurs who ran out of money and had to close their doors, how many of them do you think ran these numbers?

And what do you think would have happened if they did?

Okay, let's move on to the final week in this aspect of your 30-day challenge. Let's talk about doing some long-term planning in order to solidify your vision.

Week 4: Do Some Long-Term Planning

You now have a good idea of how much money it will take to launch your business, whether or not it is profitable enough to justify its costs, and how long you will have to work in it until you begin to see a profit.

That was a lot of work, and a bunch of numbers to crunch, wasn't it?

That's why you'll be happy to know that in this final section of the financials, I want you to put your dream cap on. I'm veering a little on how this is typically done because our purposes are so much different.

People generally do long-range planning to find out profitable the business will be in 2, 3, or even 5 years down the road, but that's not why I want you to do this exercise. Instead, I want you to create a vision for your new business, and then determine if that's the vision that will sustain you for the long road ahead.

So, here's what we're going to do. Start by taking out a notebook or open a document on your computer. Then forget about all the numbers you just crunched and think in more abstract terms.

Let's get started, shall we?

What Will Your Business/Life Look Like in a Year?

The first thing I'd like you to do is think about what your business and your life will look like a year after you open your doors. You should have some idea of how profitable it will be by then and that will help.

Here's where we'll drill down to your dreams, visions, and wishes. I'd like you to write a paragraph of how you would think your business will look in a year from now. But don't stop there—also write a paragraph about your personal life and how the business will be affecting it.

Next, I want you to take apart this paragraph and identify the positives and the negatives. Then, we'll work on how to reduce the cons and increase the pros, giving you a pathway to the vision and business you truly want to create.

For instance, our landscape guy's paragraph could look something like this:

My projections show that in a year, I will be so busy that I may need to hire 2 more crews. In the area of town that I'm targeting, 3 new subdivisions are being built, and that will result in even more business. It will mean a lot of work but it should pay off well financially.

My personal life will be very busy trying to keep up with the business. My wife will likely be supportive and upset at the same time, so I'll have to find a way to bring a real balance to keep everyone happy. I can't let my success ruin my marriage.

Now it's time to analyze the paragraphs and identify what's right and what needs to be addressed and changed. This business owner is obviously happy that his business is set to be thriving within the next year, and he will be financially comfortable. But he also wants to be able to spend time with his wife and enjoy the fruits of his labor.

Now he has to figure out how to have both worlds. The most obvious solution would be to hire a project manager to oversee the crews so the business owner could spend more time with his family. If he hires this manager as soon as the business becomes profitable, it would give him to time to train him and become comfortable with the prospect of allowing him to take over this aspect of the business. He may also consider adding another service to help justify the salary of the project manager.

Now make your projections visual. You can do this any way you like, such as using a calendar or a hand-drawn timeline. Map out the steps you'll need to take to shape your business into *your* vision and then stay on top of it all year long.

Do you see how taking a look into the future can help you shape your business as it grows so that it meets *your* expectations and stays in line with *your* vision? It's so easy to be controlled by a business, rather than you controlling it. That's why a lot of entrepreneurs burn out or lose interest in their business—it gets out-of-control and soon becomes the biggest thing in their life. And oftentimes, it's at the expense of everything else the entrepreneur loves and holds dear.

You should ultimately have a 5-year plan for your business. If you have that vision now, go ahead and repeat this process identifying the likely state of your business by then, and how it lines up with your desired lifestyle. If you can't think that far ahead, it's okay. As long as you start with a 1 year projection, you can create your 5 year plan once the first year comes to a close.

Let's Review

We've come a long way, haven't we? By now, you should have a good understanding of whether you have what it takes to run a company, and if not, you know how to make changes so that you're up to the job. You should have a clear understanding of whether your product or service is sustainable as a business, and if it isn't, you've saved yourself a lot of time and money. If it is, you now know how much it will cost to get started, what you can expect in terms of sales in the first year, when you will reach the break-even point in your business, and now you have a way to ensure that you will run business, not the other way around.

What's left?

More planning, of course! In the next chapter, I'll outline a roadmap for you to follow and bring all of this together.

Are you ready to get to the finish line? Let's do this thing!

Part Four: Putting it All Together, Creating a Roadmap for Success, and a Surprise Ending

If you've read this far, I assume that you've analyzed your strengths and weaknesses for each area. You know that you're a good fit for the entrepreneurial life, you're sure that a market exists for your product or service, you've got your financial life in line—including the means to finance your business—and you've thought long and hard about whether or not the long-term goals of the business are in line with what you want for your life.

Congratulations. If you've meticulously analyzed each of these areas and decided that you're a good fit in all of them, you probably have a winning business idea on your hands. But if you find that you're not quite up to speed in an area, please take the time to do the work until it's right before you go forward.

That's the entire point of this book, isn't it? It would easy to brush by some of the more difficult areas, but if you, do so at your own risk. Starting a business is one of the best things you can do for your future, but only if you do it right. Remember 50 percent of the people who start a business every year fail. And they fail because they brushed off the importance of one of these key areas.

If you're ready to move on, I would like to leave you with a roadmap of sorts. I find that a simple worksheet oftentimes helps people focus so I've put together one for you on the next few pages. Grab a cup of coffee, fill it out, and watch your dream go from in your head to paper.

My Roadmap to Success

1. Entrepreneurial traits to work on:

Trait:_____

Work done: _____

Date mastered: _____

Trait: _____

Work done: _____

Date mastered: _____

2. Market Research

Small Focus group date completed and lessons learned:

_____

2nd Focus group date completed and lessons learned:

_____

Prototype made or service tested and outcomes:

_____

Final focus group: date completed and lessons learned

_____

3. Finance

Total monthly personal and business expenses:

$_____

Total startup costs needed:

$_____

Preferred method of finance (date applied/approved or rejected:

_____

Second method of finance (date applied/approved or rejected:

_____

Final method of finance. (Date approved/amount):

_____

Beginning and ending credit score:

_____

Likely first year profits:

_____

Month and year business will break even:

_____

4. Long-term Planning

What my business will look like in 1 year:

_____

_____

_____

What my business will look like in 5 years:

_____

_____

_____

Is this the right time to start this business?

_____

And there you have it: a roadmap of everything you've learned in this book so you can see—in black and white—whether your business idea has merit. When you look at the facts, figures, and research, it makes it a lot easier to decide whether or not to go forward, doesn't it?

A Word about Failure

> *"Nine out of ten businesses fail; so I came up with a foolproof plan — create ten businesses."*— Robert Kiyosaki

Finally, I'd like to leave you with an unexpected ending: a word about failure. You see, most experienced entrepreneurs understand that failure is just another word for "process," and so I want to leave you with some food for thought.

You've done your research and homework, and that means you have a better chance than most for success, but no can predict the future. And so I thought I would end this book talking about failure—only I'm going to put a different spin on it than most.

Here's an interesting fact for you to absorb: People who have previously started a business and failed have a 20 percent chance of succeeding on their next venture as opposed to an 18 percent chance of success by those who are starting out for the first time. Why? Because the second time entrepreneurs likely learned the importance of the areas we talked about in this book.

Sometimes experience, even bad experience is what catapults people to the next level. But in order to grasp this concept, you must have an entrepreneurial spirt like we spoke about in part 1 of this book.

Want an example?

Kurt Theobald is an entrepreneur who didn't create a successful business until his eleventh try, and he has something interesting to say about his journey.

"I wrote two things in my journal: One, when I fall, I am getting up. Every single time. And two; I get up because it's who I am as an entrepreneur. Therefore to not get up is

to betray who I am. And so that's what kept me going through all the failure. You can't stop. You don't really have a choice because if you choose that then you might as well sacrifice your whole life."

Telling, isn't it?

It's this spirit that drives entrepreneurs and makes them who they are. And people with this spirit will succeed. It may be the first time, the second, or as in Theobald's case, the eleventh. But long-term failure is simply not an option.

It's Your Time to Shine

Now that you've done the hard work of introspection, research, and planning, it's time to go out there and pursue your dream. I'm not telling you that it's going to be easy, but now that you've put in the work, you'll have it a lot easier than most.

So, what do you think? Will you start your own business now, or did you learn that you still have some work to do before you launch?

A Personal Note

One my favorite things is keeping up with my readers and their awesome pursuits. I've heard a great many stories about people who have gone on to build amazing companies, and I would love to hear about your journey as well. If you've got some exciting news, please go to RainMakerPress.com and share it with me!

Now, go out there and pursue your dreams!

Sam

The Work from Home Series

How to Work From Home and Make Money: 10 Proven Home-Based Businesses You Can Start Today (Work from Home Series: Book 1)

Life is Too Short to Work for Someone Else!

Are you tired of struggling just to get by with a paycheck that doesn't quite stretch far enough? Or are you one of the millions of people who are out of work in an economy gone bad? Maybe you long to be your own boss so you can set your own schedule and choose the path your life will take.

Whatever it is that brought you to this page, you're obviously looking for answers. **The good news is you've come to the right place.**

I've spent the past 20 years working for myself, and I would never dream of punching another clock or trudging to someone else's office every day to collect a meager paycheck. That's because I've discovered the secret: when you work for yourself, you're happier, more productive, and you have unlimited earning potential.

After all, **why would you want to work so hard to fund someone else's dreams?**

Working for myself has allowed me to live a lifestyle that many people can only dream about. I have the flexibility to create the life I want, take days off when I need to, and I decide how much money I make by choosing the hours I work.

But don't be fooled. Working from home at a home-based business isn't easy. It takes hard work and dedication to build a successful business that will make money.

In my book, I'm pleased to offer you **10 proven, realistic ways to work from home and earn a great income.** And I won't just offer you a brief explanation of each method like some other books do.

In each chapter, I provide you with the information and facts you need to determine if that business is right for you. But I don't stop there. I'll also give you important links and resources, so if you decide you want to pursue one of the home-based business ideas listed in this book, **you'll have everything you need to begin.**

So, the choice is yours. Will you wake up tomorrow morning and spend your day funding someone else's dream, or will you finally take the steps needed to claim your own success?

Why not start right now by buying How to Work From Home and Make Money? It's one of the most important things you'll do to begin the process of achieving your own dreams.

[Click here to go to Amazon and buy the book!](#)

How to Build a Writing Empire in 30 Days or Less (Work from Home Series: Book 2)

How to Build a
WRITING
EMPIRE in
30 Days or Less

Sam Kerns

Do You Want to Make a Real Living as a Writer? You'll Have to Throw Out Everything You Know

Let me guess—you're a talented writer who is willing to do whatever it takes to make a full-time living by writing. You've read countless articles and books on the subject, followed the suggestions in them, but you just can't seem to make the income leap.

Or you may be a new writer who is convinced that you're missing something because your own experience isn't matching up to what you've read is possible.

Or perhaps you've been moonlighting as a freelance writer for years, and you're convinced that it's simply not possible to quit your "real" job and do what you love full time.

Let me tell you a secret. You've been lied to. Yes, you heard me correctly. **Lied. To.**

The truth is, only about 10 percent of writers earn enough working full time to support themselves. *Ten percent*. That's not something all those other how-to writing books spend a lot of time on, is it?

Luckily, there's a real solution.

I know this because I've been doing it myself for years. But in order to be successful in this business, you'll have to turn the current freelance writing working model on its head. In fact, you pretty much **have to throw everything you thought you knew out the window.**

What I'm talking about is a new system. One that doesn't limit a freelance writer's ability to make a great income because of time constraints. I'm talking about earning a living anyone would be proud of.

In this book, I'll show you how to create your own Writing Empire in 30 days or less. You'll learn:

- Why most freelancers can't make a decent living—and what to do about it
- How to structure your writing business in a way that works best for your lifestyle
- How to brand your business to attract the type of clients you want
- Where to find clients and how to land the jobs
- How to structure your time in order to earn the highest possible income in the shortest amount of time
- How to hire a team of qualified, motivated writers who will help you build your Empire

And that's not all. I'll give you a **step-by-step plan** that will lead you to success. This plan looks **in detail** at your first:

- Day
- Week
- Month
- And beyond

Like I said, I structured my own business this way, so let my experience help you achieve your dreams.

Are you ready to get serious about your writing career and make some serious money? Start right now by downloading the book and learn how to make a real living with writing!

Click here to buy the book on Amazon!

How to Start a Home-Based Food Business: Turn Your Foodie Love into Serious Cash with a Food Business Startup (Work from Home Series Book 3)

Finally, a Comprehensive Guide to Starting a Food Business!

Do your insides jump for joy when you see a perfectly frosted cupcake or cookie? Or do you love the look of violet lavender syrup or a mouthwatering strawberry and lime jam? Or are you more of a savory person and melt when you see a jar of homemade salsa or seasoned nuts with just the right amount of spices?

If food excites you as much as it does me, you just might be a foodie. And in today's food-centered world, there is serious money to be made with your passion.

Food consumption has really changed in the past decade, and now more than ever, people want to know what's in their food, where it came from and who made it. That's bad news for businesses that mass produce food, but great news for those in the cottage food industry.

You see, in the past individuals who wanted to sell food were required to involve the state health inspectors and lease commercial kitchens in order to sell to the public. Obviously, that prevented a lot of people from pursuing their food dreams. But now many states have passed **cottage food laws** that are designed to give home chefs and bakers the right to produce products from their homes and sell them to the public.

If you've read my other books, you know I'm a serial entrepreneur. I've opened and closed many businesses in my lifetime, and there's nothing I love more than taking an idea and turning it into a smoothly run, profitable business. And this book was born of that desire.

Let me explain.

I bake. There—it's out in the open. I'm a guy and I bake. Can we please move on?

Specifically, I bake specialty brownies that are so good I've had local stores approach me and ask me to sell them wholesale, and I get phone calls from friends begging me to bake a batch. Yeah, my brownies are that good.

So when I heard about the changes in the law allowing people to start home-based food businesses, my entrepreneurial mind starting spinning. I have a great product, so in my mind, there was no reason why I couldn't create a profitable business. I should just open one, right?

Fortunately, that's not the way I roll. I have never simply opened a business and learned as I go—instead I conduct so much research that I know absolutely everything there is to know before I begin. In other words, I leave no room for error. I want the information up front so I can make the best decisions and build a successful business.

Otherwise, what's the point?

So, when the idea of opening a cottage food business occurred to me, I began researching and I didn't stop for months. That's where this book comes in. There is a lot to know about this type of business, and one thing I learned is that there is simply nowhere that you can get all of the information in one place.

Until this book.

Don't believe me? Take a look at all the other books on the subject and just see if the author provides a state-by-state index of all the cottage food laws. Let me save you some time. They don't.

And recipes that fit into the guidelines of the laws? Nope, you won't find them in other books. How about serious insight into how to best brand, package and market your home-based food business? You'll only find that in this book.

So, let my obsessive research into business ideas, along with my entrepreneurial skills, help you in your own business. I've done the hard work for you, so **all you have do is follow the plan I've outlined in this book and you'll be on your way to building your very own food business**. And all the newbie questions you have but are too embarrassed to ask? I had them, too and I've included the answers to them in this book.

If you're ready to pursue your foodie dreams, download the book and learn everything you need to know!

Click here to buy the book on Amazon!

How to Brand Your Home-Based Business: Why Business Branding is Crucial for Even the Smallest Startups (Work from Home Series Book 4)

How to

Your Home-Based Business

Sam Kerns

What's the Difference Between a Successful Home-Based Business and One that Fails? Branding.

Home-based business startups are exploding all across the world as more and more people realize that the best way to take control of your life—and your finances—is to work for yourself. But what many people forget to do is brand their small business.

That's a mistake. You see, business branding isn't only for the big guys. Home-based business owners also need to focus on creating a brand that will speak to their customers and forge that ever-important bond between the business and the public.

But home-based business owners shouldn't play by the same rules when it comes to branding their business. For starters, most solopreneurs don't have the finances to pay big shot logo designers, graphic artists and copywriters, not to mention the cash to invest in top-notch packaging and marketing efforts.

And why would you want to?

Building a brand doesn't have to be expensive or complicated, but it does require a plan and the knowledge about how to best create the right brand and then use it to build your business.

If you own a home-based business and can't figure out why you're not meeting your goals, could it be that you haven't take the time to properly brand it? And if you're just starting out, you shouldn't even think about opening your doors until you've branded your business for success.

In this book, I'll show you:

- What branding is and why your business can't truly succeed without it
- The biggest benefits you'll reap from a business brand
- The 7 mistakes most people make when building a brand—and how to avoid them
- How to build a brand in today's high-tech world
- A step-by-step guide to brand building that will work for any type of business (along with links and resources)

Don't let your hard work go to waste. Increase your market share (and profits) in your current home-based business, or start your new business on the right foot by reading this important book.

Click Here to Buy The Book from Amazon!

The Writer's Toolkit Boxed Set (Work from Home: Books 2 and 5)

Two bestselling books in one boxed set!

Click here to buy the boxed set from Amazon!

The Weekend Writer: How to Write a Non-Fiction Book in Two Months even if You Have a Full-Time Job (Work from Home Series: Book 6)

Do you fear you'll never publish a book because you don't have time to write?

Let me guess—you're a writer, but so far, the book you *know* will be a big hit is stuck inside your head because you simply don't have the time to sit down and write it. You've probably been told that you need to block out mass chunks of time to write a book, but I'm here to tell you that's just not true.

It's possible to write a quality book in two months—writing only on the weekends—using my step-by-step plan.

I'm not talking about putting out some of the junk that passes for books these days. I'm talking about writing a full-length book you'll be proud to put your name on, and readers will be thrilled they bought.

Here's what you'll find in this revolutionary book:

- How to get in the right mindset to write on a limited schedule
- How to choose your book topic so it sells
- How to outline your book in a way that makes writing it easier
- How to set up a no-fail writing schedule so you can meet your deadline
- How to use productivity hacks that will help you stay on track and accomplish your goal
- How to edit as you go
- A weekend-by-weekend guide that shows you the exact steps you need to take to have a finished book in just two months—only writing on the weekends.

Click here to buy the book from Amazon!

How to Relaunch Your Book: Use this 7-Step Proven Program to Bring Your Book Back to Life (Book 7)

Do You Have a Book That Isn't Selling? Don't Leave Money on the Table!

There's nothing more exciting than writing and publishing a book, but if you're like most authors, your book sells for the first couple of months and then quietly and alarmingly sinks to the bottom of Amazon's rankings. Or maybe your book never saw success. There are thousands of book authors who thought their book would achieve success only to watch it sink to the bottom of the rankings. Sadly most book authors simply accept that it's just the way things are.

But it doesn't have to be.

The truth is, **it is possible to relaunch your book months—or even years—after its initial release and see success.** To prove this, I'll use the first book in my Work from Home series, and relaunch it as an example of the process I outline in this book. I purposefully allowed the book to slip in the rankings so I could use it as a case study for this book. But keep in mind that I'm certain the program works because I've used it many times.

A successful book relaunch is more complicated than simply marketing your book again. In fact, to do it successfully, you'll need to follow the 7-step program I outline in this book. Some of the things we'll cover are how to:

- Analyze your book's position
- Create an improvement roadmap
- Test the existing cover to determine whether or not to design a new one
- Rearrange your book categories using my Lift Off strategy
- Ensure your internal marketing techniques are in place to increase sales of other books in the series
- Use the relaunch to increase the size of your mailing list

- Organize the relaunch so that you don't experience another quick drop off in sales.

This book not only provides you with a 7-step process, but I'll also give you an "over the shoulder" look at how I successfully follow the program myself.

If you have books on Amazon that aren't selling, you're leaving money on the table. Why should your only option be continuously writing new books to make money on Amazon? The secret is that you can—and should—revive your old books. Won't you follow along as I show you how to bring your backlist to life and reignite those book sales?

<u>Buy the Book on Amazon!</u>

www.ingramcontent.com/pod-product-compliance
Lightning Source LLC
Chambersburg PA
CBHW071417220526
45469CB00004B/1310